EFFECTIVE
SCHOOL
LEADERSHIP

THE NATIONAL SOCIETY
FOR THE STUDY OF EDUCATION

Series on Contemporary Educational Issues
Kenneth J. Rehage, Series Editor

The 1987 Titles:

Reaching Marginal Students: A Primary Concern for School Renewal, by Robert L. Sinclair and Ward J. Ghory

Effective School Leadership: Policy and Process, John J. Lane and Herbert J. Walberg, editors

The National Society for the Study of Education also publishes Yearbooks which are distributed by the University of Chicago Press. Inquiries regarding all publications of the Society, as well as inquiries about membership in the Society, may be addressed to the Secretary-Treasurer, 5835 Kimbark Avenue, Chicago, IL 60637. Membership in the Society is open to any who are interested in promoting the investigation and discussion of educational programs.

EFFECTIVE SCHOOL LEADERSHIP

POLICY AND PROCESS

Edited by

John J. Lane
DePaul University

and

Herbert J. Walberg
University of Illinois at Chicago

McCutchan Publishing Corporation

P.O. Box 774
Berkeley, California 94701

ISBN 0-8211-1115-9
Library of Congress Catalog Card Number 86-63774

Printed in the United States of America

Contributors

Robert L. Crowson, University of Illinois at Chicago
Chad D. Ellett, Louisiana State University
Eugene E. Eubanks, University of Missouri at Kansas City
John J. Lane, DePaul University
Daniel U. Levine, University of Missouri at Kansas City
Rayna F. Levine, University of Missouri at Kansas City
Joseph Licata, Louisiana State University
R. Bruce McPherson, University of Illinois at Chicago
Van Cleve Morris, University of Illinois at Chicago
Allan Odden, University of Southern California, Los Angeles
Samuel Peng, National Institute of Education
Susan Rosenholtz, University of Illinois at Urbana-Champaign
John R. Staver, University of Illinois at Chicago
Herbert J. Walberg, University of Illinois at Chicago

Contents

1

Introduction and Overview

John J. Lane and Herbert J. Walberg

For several reasons, school effectiveness is a matter of widespread concern. In its report *A Nation At Risk*, the National Commission on Excellence in Education (1983) suggested that achievement test scores of U.S. students have been declining and compare unfavorably with those of students in other industrialized countries. Yet the percentage of all U.S. workers in the "knowledge industries"—those that produce, process, and distribute information goods and services—rose from 5 percent in 1860 to about 50 percent in 1980; and the growth sectors of the economy may require that their workers have even greater verbal, numerical, scientific, and social abilities in the future if the United States is to remain internationally competitive in the production of goods and services and in the relative quality of the lives of its citizens (Walberg 1983).

Since the commission's report, several dozen other national reports have been completed; and it has been estimated that some 350 committees of state legislatures have been considering and enacting various educational reforms (Tomlinson and Walberg 1986). Some national reports call for expanding the curriculum core of fundamental subjects and removing electives, but many educators wish to preserve the diversity of curriculum offerings. A greater consensus on national goals for education may sacrifice local autonomy and individual initiative. Achieving excellence may diminish equality of opportunity. To avoid such undesirable trade-offs—to create a rising tide that lifts all boats—educators, parents, and students can work longer and harder (National Commission 1983); but they can also work more effectively (Walberg 1983), and school principals can lead this important effort.

PURPOSE AND ORGANIZATION

The purpose of this book is to summarize and discuss recent perspectives, research, and practices related to effective administration in the context of effective schools. Neither the editors nor the chapter authors view school administration and effectiveness as matters that can be substantially improved by a single theory or practice. Rather, a complex web of economic, political, psychological, and sociological forces act upon administrators and schools. This constellation of forces requires a variety of perspectives to provide a comprehensive understanding that will lead to efficient, humane, and enduring improvements. It was in this spirit that the authors were invited to contribute their chapters.

The themes of this book are that schools can make a large difference in learning and that the administrator is a key element in school effectiveness. Having been preoccupied for more than a decade with large-scale studies of the effects of sociological and economic factors on schooling, researchers have overlooked the value of educational leadership; but the principalship is now emerging as a critical element in school effectiveness. Awareness of the principal's unique potential contribution to instructional improvement supports the expression: "Show me an effective school, and I will show you an effective principal."

In recent years millions of dollars have been spent on educational planning, curriculum development, and evaluation and on the development of such key personnel as curriculum directors, reading specialists, and special education teachers. At the same time, while expectations for principals continue to grow and change, comparatively little has been done to improve their professional performance (Lane 1984). In the past, moreover, school administrators who sought to increase their effectiveness looked beyond school research to borrow management techniques from the business world (Lane 1985). Contributors to this volume, on the contrary, are convinced that research on school effectiveness and improvement, and on effective principals, provides rich resources for upgrading the schools. Other developments raise the principalship to renewed prominence. Site-level management, for example, returns to the principal the responsibility for hiring and inducting teachers and other staff; developing the budget, curriculum, and instructional procedures; and maintaining positive community relations. And although national, state, and school-district efforts to improve education will undoubtedly continue, the school and classroom are the chief places where reforms actually take place.

The subsequent chapters in this book are divided into three parts. The chapters in the first part, "Perspectives on School Effectiveness," discuss both the philosophy underlying the purposes of schooling and the many initiatives being taken by the states to improve schools.

The chapters in the second part, "Research on Educational Effects," review syntheses of research on educational productivity and summarize research on effective elementary and secondary schools. The chapters in this part exemplify three research approaches to the establishment of principles of school effectiveness: synthesis of numerous experimental and controlled research studies, a large-scale national statistical survey, and the gleaning of information from qualitative case studies of effective programs in school systems.

The third section, "Effective Leadership," discusses what makes principals effective, their opportunities and constraints, and their promotion of positive morale within schools.

PART ONE: PERSPECTIVES ON SCHOOL EFFECTIVENESS

Two major perspectives can and should be extremely influential in determining school practices—the basic philosophical or theoretical approach to the purposes and methods of schooling and the initiatives that states (where educational reforms are initiated) are now enacting to improve schools. With respect to the first perspective, Van Cleve Morris, in "Educational Aims and the Management of Schools," identifies fundamental philosophical positions regarding the governance and operation of schools. These positions hinge on two dominant theories operating in American schools: the transmission of culture and the development of the individual student. Morris discusses how these views shape education and, more particularly, the principal's role. He introduces many of the themes taken up by the authors in their subsequent chapters.

Allan Odden, in "School Effectiveness, Backward Mapping, and State Education Policies," provides an overview of state initiatives to raise the schools to the levels of quality expected by parents and taxpayers. Using the technique of "backward mapping," which he describes in his opening section, Odden assesses how state policies are affecting local school districts and schools themselves. He reviews research on effective schools in the light of state policies and identifies several exemplary and instructive state policies.

PART TWO: RESEARCH ON EDUCATIONAL EFFECTS

Research on school effectiveness suggests more definitively than ever before that educational achievement and other outcomes can be raised significantly by systematically employing proven practices. This part of the book illustrates three approaches to establishing what works in improving school effectiveness.

In "Successful Implementation of Instruction at Inner-City Schools," Daniel Levine, Rayna Levine, and Eugene Eubanks survey effective-schools programs for inner-city areas of poverty. The programs they describe are applicable to elementary schools and, with somewhat less certainty, to secondary schools. Their discussion focuses on several related topics and themes: outcomes-based instruction; organizational arrangements for low achievers; coordination of instruction; avoidance of implementation pitfalls, particularly an overemphasis on lower-order skills; the encouragement of shared values; collegial or cooperative as contrasted to bureaucratic implementation; and selection of an overall approach. The authors provide illustrations of these concepts in various cities and show how they relate to one another.

Samuel Peng, in "Effective High Schools: What Are Their Attributes?" reports on factors that make a difference in school effectiveness as revealed by extensive analysis of data from the national survey "High School and Beyond." Among the variables that predict student achievement gains are parental encouragement and support for learning; school type, facilities, homework, and disciplinary effectiveness; the percentages of students in academic curricula; and the breadth of mathematics and science courses offered.

John Staver and Herbert Walberg, in their chapter "Educational Research and Productivity," summarize recent syntheses of research according to nine factors that consistently influence academic learning: student age, ability, and motivation; the quality and amount of instruction (including self-instruction and homework); the social-psychological environments of the home, classroom, and peer group; and the mass media (particularly television, which is negatively related to learning if it is watched more than a dozen hours a week). Although all these factors appear to be consistent and even powerful influences on learning, they vary considerably in the extent to which they can be altered by educators.

PART THREE: EFFECTIVE LEADERSHIP

The final section of the book focuses on the principal's role in creating and maintaining effective schools. Each of the chapters demonstrates that principals can make a difference in the quality of the schools.

Bruce McPherson and Robert Crowson, in "Sources of Constraints and Opportunities for Discretion in the Principalship," explore the potential for school improvement residing in the discretionary authority available to principals. In particular, they encourage principals to be not only problem solvers but also problem finders. They emphasize the principal's many opportunities to positively influence teachers who, within the current organizational structures of schools, depend upon principals to establish a climate of order and to provide the resources necessary for effective teaching. A major constraint upon the principal is the need to balance and pursue simultaneously both the organization's professed goals and its operative goals. The authors, nonetheless, show that principals have considerable discretion and opportunities for creative initiatives to make schools more effective.

Chad Ellett and Joseph Licata, in "Triangulation of Selected Research on Principals' Effectiveness," synthesize four major quantitative and case studies of effective principals by "triangulating" or checking the studies against one another to single out robust, consistent findings. They offer three central propositions from the synthesis and put forward two graphic models for organizing past findings as well as future empirical studies. The chapter shows how quantitative and qualitative research may be effectively combined to yield insights on how the work of the principal may be made more productive.

Susan Rosenholtz, in "School Success and the Organizational Conditions of Teaching," integrates many of the significant findings on the principal's role in effective schools. Principals in effective schools convey a unitary mission to improve achievement. Such principals recruit like-minded teachers, support them in their work, and monitor their progress. The work of the entire staff is not only concerted but collegial: staff members motivate one another and provide cooperation, ideas, and mutual support.

REFERENCES

Lane, John J., ed. *The Making of a Principal*. Springfield, Ill.: Charles C Thomas, 1984.

Lane, John J., ed. *Management Techniques for School Districts*. Reston, Va.: International Association of School Business Officials, 1985.

National Commission on Excellence in Education. *A Nation At Risk: The Imperative for Educational Reform*. Washington, D.C.: U.S. Government Printing Office, 1983.

Tomlinson, Tommy, and Walberg, Herbert J., eds. *Academic Work and Educational Excellence: Raising Student Productivity*. Berkeley, Calif.: McCutchan Publishing Corporation, 1986.

Walberg, Herbert J. "Scientific Literacy and Economic Productivity in International Perspective." *Daedalus* 112 (Spring 1983): 1–28.

I

Perspectives on School Effectiveness

2

Educational Aims and the Management of Schools

Van Cleve Morris

INTRODUCTION

Educators have known for a long time that a relationship exists between the aims of education and the conduct of schooling. What is to be learned and how it is to be taught are both governed by the educator's ultimate purpose in shaping the young. Accordingly, most teacher-training programs include a systematic study of the aims of education, from Plato to Skinner. Such study may take the form of examining the social and political purposes of education in different kinds of society; or at a deeper level it may focus on fundamental philosophies of education and the metaphysical and epistemological views of competing schools of thought. The general intent of these studies is to provide teachers with a grounding in educational theory in order that their instructional practice in the classroom will be informed, consistent, and conceptually coherent.

In this chapter we raise a related question: If there is a connection between educational theory and classroom instruction, is there also a connection between educational theory and the management of the school as an organization? To be more explicit, if the teacher's behavior inside the classroom is guided by educational purposes, is the principal's behavior throughout the school building similarly guided by these same purposes? If so, how are these purposes revealed in the managerial conduct of the school principal, and how does administrative behavior vary from one theory to another?

If you, the reader, have already leafed through this volume or consulted the table of contents, you have noticed that the authors explore different dimensions of administrative practice as they relate to school effectiveness. In Part Three the discussion focuses directly on effective principals, examining the question, What principaling behavior has the most *effect* on teaching and learning?

As a prologue to these latter discussions, we ask here how principaling is affected by theory, and specifically how principaling behavior differs between the two dominant theories operating in American schools today:

—The school's job is to transmit the culture.
—The school's job is to develop the individual.

For each theory we first set forth the basic argument. Then we take up the type of school management best suited to the theory. Finally, we turn directly to the administrative behavior of the principal and examine how this style of leadership would manifest itself in a real school.

TRANSMITTING THE CULTURE: THE ROLE OF MANAGEMENT

The Basic Argument

Perhaps the most widely accepted purpose of education is to transmit the basic skills of living and the inherited understandings of the world we live in. Every culture, it is argued, becomes self-conscious of its own history and wishes to pass on to each succeeding generation a working understanding of its central traditions. Moreover, it wishes to equip each new member with the practical knowledge required for adaptation to the adult society. In our own case in the United States, this obligation takes the form of passing on the Western tradition as it has been handed down to us for the last 2,500 years since its origins in Greek antiquity.

In the course of this lengthy history, we have learned a great deal about the world and about ourselves. We have accumulated this learning in our libraries; scholars and specialists have summarized, interpreted, and condensed it into our encyclopedias. Much of what we have learned about the world has, of course, turned out to be wrong, and that is why we maintain colleges, universities, and a free press so that error can be eliminated wherever we find it. What manages to survive this ongoing critique is our best version of truth in the contemporary world, and each edition of the encyclopedia attempts to present that truth as accurately as possible.

The school's curriculum might be thought of as a further condensation of the accumulated knowledge and wisdom of twenty-five centuries of Western learning; we typically know it as the subject-matter curriculum in which all the major areas of knowledge have been systematically separated and arranged in learnable segments. The first task of the school is to transmit this material to each newcomer to our society.

This view was succinctly summarized some years ago by John Ciardi, former poetry editor of the *Saturday Review* and general man of letters. In addressing an incoming class of freshmen at Rutgers University (Ciardi 1954, pp. 2–3), he spoke of the famous names carved in the friezes of the university's buildings: persons of science, literature, politics, and the arts. "You," he said, "probably will not get your name carved there; but you already know more than what they knew. You have been going to school now for thirteen years, and you have been learning what they left behind." The first business of the student, he said, is "to learn what the past has already learned for you."

In a similar vein, William Bennett, Secretary of Education in the second Reagan administration, put it this way:

> We should want every student to know how mountains are made, and for most actions there is an equal and opposite reaction. They should know who said "I am the state" and who said "I have a dream." They should know about subjects and predicates, about isosceles triangles and ellipses. They should know where the Amazon flows, and what the First Amendment means. They should know about the Donner Party and slavery, and Shylock, Hercules and Abigail Adams, where Ethiopia is, and why there is a Berlin Wall.

They should know a little of how a poem works, how a plant works, and what "if wishes were horses, beggars would ride" means. They should know the place of the Milky Way and DNA in the unfolding of the universe. They should know something about the Convention of 1787 and about the conventions of good behavior. They should know a little of what the Sistine Chapel looks like and what great music sounds like. (Bennett 1985)

This theory of education has been spelled out in a number of documents over the last fifty years, but perhaps its most explicit contemporary articulation is to be found in Mortimer Adler's *The Paideia Proposal* (1982). In this volume Adler and his associates specify the basic understandings, communication skills, and habits of critical judgment that every student should be expected to acquire in thirteen years of schooling. Moreover, says Adler, there is nothing in this catalogue of requirements that cannot be met in some legitimate way by every American youngster.

In a generic sense, this theory of education is no stranger to contemporary research into teaching and learning. For example, Benjamin Bloom's concept of "mastery learning," which has had such an impact on curricular design in Chicago and other cities, presumes that the business of education is to dispense the basic subject matters in such a way that each student can master them (Bloom 1976). Agreeing with Adler, Bloom asserts that his research shows that there is no such thing as a poor learner. There are only fast and slow learners. All youngsters are capable of mastering the entire K–12 curriculum, given enough time and special help from their teachers. This is a sweeping claim, and Bloom may be right; but it is important to see that he works from a basic philosophic assumption concerning the ultimate aim of education—mastery of the inherited content of subject-matter knowledge.

School Management and the Subject Curriculum

Given this general orientation, the school's day-to-day operation will reveal a programmatic consistency. The school's work will be organized by departments, representing the differentiated subject matters. The faculty will be identified with these departments as specialists in each field. Some subject matters, and therefore departments, will be considered more important and essential than others and accordingly will enjoy higher priority in the scholastic "pecking order." In most schools governed by "transmit-the-culture" advocates, the departments of English and mathematics are preeminent. These subject matters are generally considered the entryway to all other school learning, and more instructional time is devoted to them than to any other subject. Their mastery is the first business of the student.

To facilitate the dispensing of subject matter, the school building is physically structured for efficiency, with self-contained classrooms set in series on both sides (egg-crate fashion) of long corridors, each room equipped with a closable, even lockable door. Separate up and down staircases regulate the flow of student traffic between classrooms at the preprogrammed ringing of bells for the start and end of class periods. The hierarchy of management is architecturally verified by the positioning of a "central office," the administrative center from which radiate the instructions to staff and students.

The management of the school will require rational schedules of learning periods, arranged through the day so that all subjects can systematically be made available to the learner. This means that subject matter must be broken down into learnable units and lesson plans so that they conform to the daily schedule—conventionally segments of twenty to forty-five minutes for each subject, increasing in length with the age and therefore the attention span of the learner. The coordination of this schedule understandably becomes a high priority for the manager, since it is the institutional vehicle through which the school delivers its "product" of subject-matter material to the "client."

The management of the schedule must take into account not only the movements and attention spans of the learners but also the working patterns of the teachers. The principal as manager must make certain that each teacher's teaching assignment matches his or her specialized training so that pupils are provided knowledgeable instruction in every field. Ancillary professional roles are differentiated and explicitly defined—librarians, reading specialists, department heads, psychologists—and the principal must orchestrate questions of "turf" and broker "territorial" disputes as these specialists interact with the classroom teaching staff.

In addition, the principal must see to it that the teacher's systematic imparting of subject matter is not impeded by interruptions or compromised by irregularities of scheduling. From time to time, learning outside the school building will be provided in field trips, but for the most part the subject-matter curriculum is most efficiently imparted within the school's walls, in a regularized pattern of classes, arranged in a logical sequence of units, from simple to complex, and taught by didactic procedures.

Since the mastery of each subject matter by the learner is the primary datum by which a school's success is measured, the administrator must make certain that tests and examinations in each of the subjects are systematically administered at scheduled times during the school year. A pupil's failure to reach a specified level in any examination is taken as prima facie evidence that he or she has not successfully completed the teaching-learning episode. In any event, since subject-matter mastery is the decisive factor, the pupil must repeat the instruction until a satisfactory level has been reached.

The Principal's Managerial Behavior

School administration involves the principal with several distinct constituencies: teachers, students, parents, hierarchical superiors, and sometimes other groups. What impact does the transmit-the-culture theory have on the principal's relationships with these groups?

Teachers

It is evident that the first consideration in employing a new teacher is his or her subject-matter competence. Coupled with that primary criterion is the individual's ability to impart that knowledge to youngsters and to engender mastery of his or her own discipline. Although instruction may be monitored and supervised, the bottom line of teacher effectiveness is student mastery of the material; on this criterion teachers will eventually be judged. Indeed, the principal will also be evaluated, in the long run, by how well students in his or her school perform on nationally normed achievement and aptitude examinations.

In schools governed by this theory, the curriculum will remain relatively constant from year to year. Curriculum-planning groups are not necessary, and for this reason the teaching staff will have little responsibility for determining what is to be taught from year to year. This also applies, of course, to the principal for whom programmatic concerns are minimal. The inherited knowledge of the past, after all, is well codified and organized in the familiar subject-matter curriculum, and it does not have to be reshuffled and tinkered with each September.

Students

The principal's relationship with students is primarily an impersonal, institutional one. The center of the school's work is subject matter, and the student's responsibility is well marked out and understood by all. Accordingly, the principal's first concern about any student is whether he or she is achieving mastery of the material at the specified pace of instruction. As the school's executive, the principal customarily exerts a powerful influence in urging youngsters to higher levels of effort and attainment in working at their studies; indeed, in much of the literature on school effectiveness a prominent item is the degree to which the principal engenders an ambience of hard work, self-discipline, and subject-matter mastery among the student body.

In such a school, extracurricular activities are often encouraged, but the primary emphasis is on those pursuits capable of enhancing the traditional values of the culture: strengthening the competitive drive in athletics or in chess tournaments, cultivating artistic expression in dramatic and musical productions, sharpening verbal skills in debating societies or the school newspaper.

Parents

Since the aim of schooling is clear-cut and unambiguous, the principal's encounter with parents will typically concern the student's progress in the program. If parents are consulted regarding the student's behavior in the school, remediation strategies will reveal the principal's primary concern for maintaining an undisturbed learning atmosphere for other students, and for eventually socializing the offending student into the forms of decorum necessary for systematic learning.

In its extreme form the transmit-the-culture theory takes little heed of the student's motivation for learning. The subject matter is laid out in advance to be learned, and the principal must convey to the parent that "applying oneself" to the task of mastering it is the responsibility of the student. Accordingly, principals have the easiest time with parents who have, at home, already instilled in their children a *desire to learn*. Indeed, one of the prevailing assumptions of this theory is that the home environment is expected to yield this kind of pupil. This means that the principal's major administrative problem concerns those students whose home life has not provided this incentive, who simply do not want to learn, and who, for lack of interest, simply stop learning, turn to disrupting the teaching process, or, worse, drop out of school altogether. For this portion of the student body the principal may invoke the parents' help, but if that does not avail, then the principal is forced to deliver a final judgment to the parents, namely, that the student is no longer welcome in the school. This placing of responsibility for wanting to learn on the student is a leitmotif of most transmit-the-culture literature, and finds articulate expression in Theodore Sizer's *Horace's Compromise* (1984).

Hierarchical Superiors

As noted earlier, the measure of a school principal is his or her ability to "produce results," namely, reading and mathematics scores and general achievement scores at or above grade level. Of course, as in any organization, the chief executive wants the middle manager (the principal) to keep problems off the superintendent's desk and, in Navy lingo, to "run a taut ship." But this typically means not merely the absence of problems bouncing up the chain of command, but bottom-line delivery of the school's "product," that is, mastery of the curriculum. Under the aegis of this kind of superintendent, a principal would never be fired, reassigned, or bumped back to the classroom if his or her school consistently showed acceptable pupil performance levels. Complaints against a principal from teachers, students, or parents would have little credit with a superintendent if the principal can deliver, year after year, solid evidence that students are learning the curriculum.

DEVELOP THE INDIVIDUAL: THE ROLE OF MANAGEMENT

The Basic Argument

During the early twentieth century the educational community began to question the practical promise and even the theoretical soundness of the transmit-the-culture thesis. An increasing proportion of school-age youngsters was attending school and spending more years there as compulsory attendance laws began to exert their full effect. Under the impact of this Jacksonian "education-for-all" phenomenon, it became increasingly evident that the desire to learn was not distributed evenly in the population. Many students found the task of learning established subject matter both tedious and pointless, or, in today's phrase, not *relevant* to their life plans.

Moreover, there was a growing tension among educational scholars concerning the overall social yield of this theory. John Dewey in particular led the way in challenging the wisdom of the traditional view. What the world needs more of, he said in effect, is not more and more walking encyclopedias, people who have mastered the extant knowledge of Western civilization, but rather individuals who can *use* knowledge, put it to work in the world of ordinary experience, and harness its power in solving problems of the modern age. Dewey avoided terms like *reason, intellect,* or *mastery*—terms dear to the traditionalist. Instead, he said, what we are after is *intelligence*, defined generally as the capacity to apply ideas to life. If an idea can be shown to have a practical effect in everyday experience (as Charles Peirce and William James had said), then it is worth learning and using. If an idea has no such effect, then it is suitable only for pedagogues and intellectuals who make their living toying with what Whitehead called "inert" ideas.

The educational impact of this epistemological revolution was simply this: Boys and girls in school should not be put to the sterile task of learning all the subject matters of the world unless the mastery of these materials can be shown to provide practical guidance in some life activity. (For example, instruction in arithmetic customarily concludes with the required study of the division of fractions; how often in real life are we called on to perform this function?) The real business of education is to cultivate in each youngster what Dewey called "trained intelligence," the disciplined ability to put thinking at the service of the enterprises of life—personal, social, political, technological. The sterility of the traditional curriculum cannot deliver this. What is needed is a curriculum in which the student learns subject matter in the act of *using* it to understand some feature of today's world.

The emergence and gradually increasing acceptability of this view has been revealed in many public pronouncements through the years. In the 1920s and 1930s the Progressive Education Association called on educators to "join the twentieth century." They were summoned to bring their work into line with the "progress" theme of American technology in the industrial world and social reform in political and economic affairs. In 1938 the National Education Association promulgated four purposes of education: self-realization, human relationship, economic efficiency, and civic responsibility (Educational Policy Commission 1938, p. 47). Note how different these goals are from the traditional purposes. They are oriented not to the Western tradition of formal learning but to the development of the individual in a social context. As goals, they reveal a conspicuous shift *away from* a preoccupation with inherited knowledge ("what the past has learned for you") and *toward* knowledge for practical use in contemporary life.

In the 1950s, an obsession with "Life Adjustment Education" swept through the pedagogical community. The idea was to equip each youngster with the skills—intellectual, social, cognitive, behavioral—to function effectively in a fluid, changing, skill-intensive society. Simultaneously, Theodore Brameld (1956) was reviving George Counts's idea that the school was capable of "building a new social order" (Counts 1932). We are too accepting of social wrong, too acquiescent to the pernicious persistence of poverty, suffering, racial and class injustice. There is, it was argued, more inequity of income in the late 1950s than ever before, even after twenty-five years of the New and Fair Deals. If politics cannot reform America, then the schools must.

It was clear from the Dewey-Brameld line of argument that the school's curriculum and its pedagogical methodology would have to abandon didactic teaching and mastery learning as the central strategy. What was needed was a mode of instruction that would begin with problems and end with solutions plus new problems. Along the way, the learner would master, in the context of *use*, those subject matters that made a difference in the way life was lived. Delivering on Dewey's thesis of "trained intelligence," the school would now be called on to cultivate in the youngster a social imperative, namely, *problem-solving ability*. As it turned out, this new educational objective fit nicely with the scientific methodology increasingly coming to dominate American life. Indeed, "problem solving" is simply another, less presumptuous synonym for the grand rubric of "scientific method." Thus, epistemology and pedagogy joined hands. The procedure of the experimental scientist is reenacted and replicated in the classroom, albeit at less sophisticated levels.

William Heard Kilpatrick called it "the project method," in which the child's natural curiosities would be converted into researchable problems; in this method the teacher would function not as a dispenser of knowledge but rather as a "research director," and the learners would function as "research associates." The school's curriculum was thus reconstructed into a variety of *investigations*, each growing naturally out of the learners' experience. In keeping with the spirit of this kind of curriculum design, the instructional method focuses on *systematic inquiry* and *reflective thinking*.

School Management and the "Problems" Curriculum

It is evident at the outset that the demands on school administration change dramatically under the requirements of this theory of education. Teaching and learning become much more fluid, spontaneous, and inquiry centered. The daily rhythm of management is no longer governed by the orderliness and discipline provided by the subject curriculum. The school changes its function from being the curator of inherited knowledge, the protector and dispenser of the "precious cargo" of the Western tradition, to becoming the nurturing agency for the development—cognitive and social—of the client-customer. Accordingly, the administrator's attention shifts from objective subject matter to growing, maturing human beings.

The administrator's bottom-line criterion for the effectiveness of the school is no longer centered on mastery of content; rather, the administrator's "effectiveness index" becomes something not so easily measured but nevertheless more central to learning, namely, the growth and development of youngsters in problem-solving ability and the application of learning to life.

Most important, the interests and the curiosities of the learner move into a position of central importance. Since projects and investigations are the meat of the curriculum, and since projects drawn from the experience of the learners themselves are pedagogically the most viable and productive, the administrator must encourage the teachers to build their classroom activities around the day-to-day concerns of their students. How does the history teacher best cultivate the historiographic sense in the young mind? Instead of students' mastering the details of the American colonial period, perhaps a more pregnant point of departure would be a project in which they trace the history of their own town or city. As John Dewey once remarked, "the true starting point of history is always some present situation with its problems" (Dewey 1916, p. 251). Biology can be learned starting with the basic rubrics of genus and species. But perhaps the study of biology should begin at the other end of the spectrum, where it touches the lives of people. A study of a common housefly or the family dog would soon elicit the need for wider understanding of biological forms, but would do so from an origin of active, personal interest.

It is true that in compiling an encyclopedia (or a subject-matter curriculum), it makes sense to present information in a logical form. But in a pedagogical situation, the learning mind takes hold of information in what Dewey called the "psychological" mode, close to the experience of that mind. Hence, in the art of pedagogy, where the teacher begins is a critical variable.

The instructional schedule, so rationalized and codified in a subject-matter school, becomes a more flexible vehicle in a problems-centered school. The administrator must enable teachers to change direction, to turn their teaching impromptu toward events of the day, so as to capture the natural excitement of learners. This means that the administrator must become the arranger of field trips outside the school, of transfers of pupils from one class to another, of adjustments of pupils with different teachers. The managerial sphere of activity expands to include changes in schedule, visitors brought in to enhance instruction, and, in our own day, special accommodations for handicapped youngsters, bilingual programs, and learners with varying learning speeds.

The ideas that there is one curriculum for everybody and that every child can master it in its entirety are surrendered in favor of a more free-flowing school day in which boys and girls work on activities of their own choosing and the teacher functions as the investigation guide and resource specialist.

In such a school, teachers leave the cloister of their "own" classrooms and join with other staff members in team-teaching arrangements. The ambience of instruction is characterized by openness, flexibility, and movement. Students flow from one activity to another, as their investigations require. Doors are unlocked and open, or they disappear altogether in the building architect's blueprints. School management becomes less geographically centralized, with the principal and assistants conducting the managerial function throughout the building at the work stations of other people.

As the "develop-the-individual" theory of education has gained increasing acceptance, educators have understandably gravitated to life outside the school for educational experiences. The so-called "real world" of adults becomes an extension of the classroom, which means that youngsters not only take field trips to observe what is going on there, but participate directly in the work of the wider community as a part of their education. Thus, students study the world of work in a part-time job or apprentice themselves in nursing or auto mechanics by spending their after-school hours in hospitals or repair shops.

These outside-the-school activities are "learning laboratories" for students, but they also serve as motivating devices to enable youngsters to test their skills where they will actually be used. The importance of these activities in the educational program is generally acknowledged in "develop-the-individual" programs. But if they are important, then someone must be assigned the task of creating and managing them. Thus, the administrator is forced to assume an additional role, namely, as arranger and coordinator of ad hoc, community-based activities for each student. With this added responsibility, the administrator becomes less and less an educational leader and more and more a coordinating manager of a complex operation that requires minute-to-minute surveillance and orchestration.

Almost all recent studies of school administration at the site level have commented on the principal as "the peripatetic problem solver," the executive who is physically in motion during most of his or her managerial day and who administers the school by a series of one-on-one conversations, one after another, at classroom doorways or corridor stop-off places (Morris, Crowson, Hurwitz, and Porter-Gehrie 1984). The most plausible explanation for this phenomenon is the gradual shift in focus of administration from subject matter to people. As a school becomes less knowledge-centered and more learner-centered, the principal's role will increasingly become that of "the moving problem-solver" who spends more than half the time outside his or her suite of offices.

As noted in the previous section, the principal in a transmit-the-culture school is oriented to requirements of the curriculum, the expectations of performance by teachers and students, and the enforcement of rules, regulations, and procedures. In the develop-the-individual theory the principal is oriented to the solving of problems and the creation of a healthy social ambience inside the school building.

The Principal's Managerial Behavior

Here again, we wish to trace the principal's relationship with several constituencies. How does the develop-the-individual theory of education influence the principal in going about his or her daily tasks?

Teachers

In the hiring of teachers under this theory, the first consideration is not how well grounded the applicants are in a designated discipline but how successful they are, or have been, in motivating youngsters to the investigative mode of learning. Can prospective teachers arouse the curiosities of youngsters, can they get inquiry started, and can they lead youngsters in an active pursuit of fuller understanding of some problem or concern with which the students themselves identify? It is obvious that documentary evidence of such skill is not easy to obtain. But an indirect measure might be the intellectual curiosity of the teacher candidate. Does this person have an inquisitive mind—about the school, about the community, about what the morning newspaper had to say about national events? An applicant's active curiosity about life in general may be a tip-off that he or she would be a good choice for the position.

Once the teacher is on the job, the reward system continues consistent with selection criteria: can the teacher get youngsters excited about learning, arouse their interest, even their passion, for knowing more about some sphere of life, and sustain that eagerness to learn through the episodes of research, writing, and reporting to the class on what they have found? Over the years, as the principal steps into the classroom, he or she will be able to tell whether this ability is present, and in what degree.

In schools with a focus on problem solving and inquiry, the curriculum (as noted above) becomes a moving catalogue of investigations. Under the aegis of this theory, curriculum decision making is a continuing activity. Accordingly, one of the principal's main functions is coordinating and leading teacher groups in regular reviews of curriculum patterns. Since different patterns require different materials, equipment, and instructional arrangements, the principal is expected to provide for these pattern-specific requirements.

In any school that is more person oriented than subject-matter oriented, the principal will have more frequent occasion to call on teachers for advice on handling problems with pupils or other teachers. Conflict resolution is now a major responsibility of the effective administrator, and the consultative principal, seeking the fullest knowledge of interpersonal relationships before making decisions, is likely to have more frequent and regular contact with the teaching staff, often on matters not related to the educational program.

Students

In a develop-the-individual school, the principal is understandably interested in students less as "mastery machines" than as persons developing the ability to use knowledge in their own lives. Although personal friendship is appropriately rare in principal-student relations, nevertheless the principal *qua* school leader may take an active interest in how the student is responding to school work and how well the student pursues investigative inquiry in his studies. So far as the principal is concerned, the failing student is not the one who cannot master the material, but rather the one whose interest and curiosity cannot be aroused for active, involved school study. This is the youngster the principal concentrates on to determine what the school may be failing to do in bringing this individual into the school's orbit of problem-solving activities.

Parents

In the conventional wisdom of American life, the family historically has been responsible for developing the individual. To the traditional parent, therefore, the school's participation in this may seem somewhat unfamiliar. At the same time, most parents want their children to learn not only the basic knowledges of the world but how to put those knowledges to work for their own advancement later on in adult society. They expect the school to perform this function, since they as parents are typically not equipped to do it themselves. The principal, accordingly, must socialize the parents into an understanding of the school's role in this endeavor and explain how the school's instructional program—both within and outside the school walls— contributes to their child's maturation and intellectual development.

Understandably, in a person-oriented theory, the principal will be attentive to how well the parents' child is adjusting to the schools' social environment, since social development, as well as intellectual and cognitive growth, is a school concern. For example, a child's antisocial behavior becomes the agenda for principal-parent conferences.

According to both the person-oriented theory and the transmit-the-culture theory, the principal values parents who deliver to the school youngsters who have an active desire to learn. If anything, schools following the person-oriented theory rely even more heavily on this factor since investigative, problem-solving learning depends ultimately on the natural curiosity of the learner. Hence, the most difficult problems for a principal vis-à-vis parents are those students whose curiosity levels are consistently low but who cannot be excluded from school on that account. The principal and parents must devote their greatest ingenuity to these cases.

Hierarchical Superiors

It was noted in the discussion of the transmit-the-culture theory that the principal's effectiveness on the job is measured eventually by the year-to-year mastery of content of the students enrolled in the school, a measure that is typically easy to obtain. No such clearly defined "bottom-line" criterion is available in a school driven by problem-solving concepts and a concern for the individual child. Like the principal who must judge teachers, the superintendent must judge the effectiveness of a principal on how active and vibrant are the learning activities under way in the principal's school. This is likely to require that the superintendent conduct a periodic tour through the school in order to witness personally the level of excitement and the quality of problem solving exhibited by the students. In general, the successful develop-the-individual principal has fewer dropouts, fewer "push-outs," fewer suspensions and expulsions than less effective colleagues. He or she has less vandalism, less graffiti, more school pride and spirit than other principals. Students like to come to school every morning, and teachers look forward to coming to work. If the superintendent can pick up these signals—from youngsters, teachers, parents, and other school personnel—chances are that a good, effective principal is at the helm.

SOME OTHER ADMINISTRATIVE STYLES

In the plural, variegated texture of American educational life, it is inevitable that school administration, like schools themselves, would exhibit some deviations from the preceding two strategies. As noted earlier, educational aims and purposes vary widely in American communities, and it is important to take note of some of these other administrative responses to ideological values. Although they do not stem from widely held educational theories, the following approaches nevertheless represent idiosyncratic preferences that enjoy a basic legitimacy in American life and depict how some school administrators choose to go about their jobs.

The Military Principal: The Boot Camp Style

During the nineteenth century it was widely believed that schools had something to do with the shaping of character. Although there was never clear agreement on just what "character" meant, it was generally thought to bear some relationship to moral development and the acquisition of rudimentary social responses such as respect for authority and obedience to one's elders. During the first half of the twentieth century this linkage of schools with character building seemed to diminish. Not only were schools less and less responsible for moral and ethical teaching, but the wider society itself seemed to lose interest in this sphere of social development. Morals are for religion to deal with; leave the matter to the churches. Or, morals are learned at home; let the family take care of them. In any event, educators washed their hands of this responsibility, insisting that "you can't teach morals."

Nevertheless, if character has a behavioral side, it must show itself in observable conduct—self-discipline, orderliness of work habits, subjugation of personal desires for the common good, acceptance of authority, and gracious acknowledgement of the demands of institutions and organizations that govern American social life. And, it was argued, this behavioral side most definitely *can* be taught in schools.

The military academy is perhaps the most explicit manifestation of this idea. In schools of this sort there may be a secondary interest in "transmitting the culture," and even a nod in the direction of cultivating problem-solving skills and social rapport with one's fellow citizens. But the overarching educational purpose is the shaping of behavior consistent with personal responsibility and public duty. In such schools the curriculum may be taught with vigor, but the regimen of a controlled life, from dawn to dusk, is the real teacher. Through closely monitored activities—classroom recitations, dining hall decorum, calisthenics on the playing field, and regulated study periods—the school instills in the student the personal discipline considered noble and right for a life of maximum productivity and self-control.

The principal of such an establishment is dedicated to the principles associated with such an education, and will gather faculty that will collaborate in this kind of "character training." Although not necessarily a cold martinet in the "marine sergeant" sense, the principal nevertheless must be considered the "keeper of the keys" of the moral tradition, and as such must maintain a pedagogical and institutional standard among both faculty and student body. Typically, administration of such a school is depersonalized and business-like, and it places little stress on the affective side of students' development and is more concerned with their habituation into the norms of conduct essential for a well-governed life. Moreover, the principal must personify these values in his own life, offering himself as a paradigm of the disciplined and well-tempered persona after which students (and staff) should model themselves.

Environmental Reinforcement: The Walden Two Style

By the late 1980s the name of B. F. Skinner became widely recognized in homes as well as in schools. This Harvard psychologist originally was intent on developing a new psychology that originated in, but went far beyond, the work of the Russian physiologist Ivan Pavlov and the American behaviorist John B. Watson. Beginning with a realist metaphysics, which views the world, including man, as a huge machine driven by natural laws, Skinner proposed that we abandon the dead-end notion of stimulus-response psychology. In its place, he said, we should concentrate not on what happens before behavior occurs (stimulus) but on what happens *after* it occurs (reinforcement of the environment). Specifically, what is it in the environment that is associated with the repetition of a certain form of behavior, or coordinately, what environmental conditions are connected with a particular behavior being "extinguished"? If we could identify these environmental factors and "engineer" their occurrence, we would be in a position to modify behavior along lines of our choosing.

This means that the educator should not try to change behavior directly but rather should try to change the environmental conditions in which pupils and students learn. Manipulate these conditions in a certain way and desirable behavior will follow; manipulate them again and undesirable behavior will gradually disappear. Thus "environmental engineering" becomes the new pedagogical art form, replacing didactic imparting of subject matter of the transmit-the-culture advocate and problem-solving investigations of the develop-the-individual advocate.

In one sense, the boot camp style discussed in the previous section is a special instance of Skinnerean theory. The military academy structures the environment in such a way that particular forms of behavior are rewarded and reinforced. Over time, the target behavior patterns are fixed in the student, not by haranguing him and correcting him, but by creating conditions in which certain forms of conduct are naturally encouraged and recognized as proper.

But reinforcement principles can be just as easily directed at other forms of behavior management; indeed, according to Skinner, any kind of society could theoretically be developed using these principles. Give me the behavior you want to see more of, he says, and I will arrange the environment so that these behavior patterns will gradually emerge as the dominant patterns of the culture. Let me know what behaviors you don't like, and I will manipulate the environment so that they will gradually be extinguished.

Although Skinner has outlined these ideas in many places and has written a short novelette (Skinner 1948) on their application to utopian reform, their value for us in the present discussion concerns the management of a school devoted to this educational strategy. The principal of such a school would concentrate not on mastery learning (transmit the culture) but on *behavior*; the principal's attention would be fixed not on problem-solving skill (develop-the- individual) but on *behavior*; the principal would not get distracted by an abstract term like "character" (the military principal) but would engender moral uplift and a sense of responsibility by modifying *behavior*. If orderly conduct in the classroom is desired, let the teacher recognize and reinforce it. If graffiti is a problem, don't scold the perpetrators; rather, remove the conditions that make it possible by covering the walls with paint that cannot be written on.

In the pedagogical arena, recognize and applaud right answers. Ignore wrong answers. If successful test-taking behavior is the objective, give tests. But when they have been graded, ignore the incorrect responses and concentrate on the correct responses. On the playing field, remove the mean-spirited player and isolate him; when the others exhibit acts of good sportsmanship, recognize and reward them.

The principal's relationship with teachers is governed by this same premise. When witnessing good teaching in action, give recognition to it, take an interest in it, discuss with the teacher how well he or she is doing; when poor teaching is in progress, wait until the teacher does something right, and then reward him or her for it.

The Pastoral Principal: The I-Thou Style

In the last century American education has been turned into a big business; we sometimes speak of "the education industry" because the task is so large and the procedures are driven by organizational requirements. Responding to the production-line environment in which they are forced to work, American educators have depersonalized and objectified their daily encounters with youngsters, if for no other reason than "to get the job done." The "Mr. Chips" approach to school teaching simply does not work any more. Accordingly, as enrollments have increased and curriculum strategies have become standardized and routinized, teachers have lost touch with the persons in front of them; teachers do not have time to become "friends" with their students, to listen to their inner lives and to share their personal joys and heartbreaks. As a result, the typical K–12 educational program does not touch the affective, emotional, personal evolution of the young person being inducted into a tough-minded, hi-tech culture.

Apparently, the school's demonstrated lack of interest in humanistic concerns is not lost on our young people. After they leave school, they turn in increasing numbers to what might be called the "search-for-self" industry. During their twenties especially, young adults are drawn to weekend retreats, encounter groups, "est," "rolfing," transcendental meditation, and other variations in the private-enterprise market for providing self-identifying experiences. The paperback book shelves supply a never-ending list of titles on "erroneous zones," "being your own best friend," and quasi-professional treatments of "getting in touch with your feelings." Apparently, some educational need is not being met.

Recognizing this, many principals have taken to what might be termed the "pastoral" role of the school administrator. Standing apart from daily classroom contact with students and relieved of the teacher-student, that is, judge-judgee relationship, some principals find that they are able to supply the "adult friendship" that many elementary and secondary students seem to need. In special instances, such principals may come to treat their student body as their "flock," a group of individuals who from day to day need support, encouragement, or at least a friendly ear.

Most principals enjoy the challenge of administration. But at the same time, they claim that they miss the classroom; there is a personal nostalgia for more regular contact with young people. Thus the pastoral motif in some principals' styles may come as much from a need for self-fulfillment as from a desire to be of friendly assistance to schoolchildren. In the "I-Thou" psychic embrace, as Martin Buber (1958) described it, both parties benefit, both parties grow, both parties feel more fully human.

In recent decades the philosophy of existentialism has given birth to the ancillary field of phenomenology. Without forcing the comparison too much, it could be said that the I-Thou principal helps the youngster focus on his own "phenomenology," namely, his own identity as a person, his perception of what the world expects of him, what he can contribute to it, and how he can grow in personal responsibility to meet this definition of self as he grows into adult-hood.

SCHOOL ADMINISTRATION AND THE ENDS OF EDUCATION

In this chapter we have taken a look at two dominant theories of education—"transmit the culture" and "develop the individual." Whether aware of it or not, school principals represent in their own thinking some blend of these two orientations. The argument presented here is that this intellectual affinity toward one or the other of these two polarities, or a combination of them, flows into managerial behavior as the principal moves about the building during the regular school day. As noted, the task of principaling in today's schools is a fractionated routine of personal encounters with office staff, teachers, pupils, parents, and superiors. The work day is a series of one-on-one conversations of short duration with many different individuals. The sum total of these interchanges is what we mean by school administration. The texture, complexion, and rhythm of these episodes is necessarily shaped by the principal's interpretation of the job; and this interpretation is necessarily a function of the goals the principal is working toward.

We have also examined three other configurations of principaling—the "boot camp" style, the "Walden Two" style, and the "I-Thou" style. These modes of leadership may not represent major theoretical positions; rather, they can be seen as idiosyncratic variations on the themes of educational administration that have developed in American society. As such, they constitute legitimate paradigms of the leadership principle as it finds expression in institutional life.

Like all educators, the school administrator is responsible for an institutional process that has a purpose. The way this job is performed necessarily connects with what that purpose is. Most principals report experiencing an end-of-the-day reverie, in which they make mental note of their level of job satisfaction as they head for the parking lot. "Was I an effective principal today?" The answer can be found in how close a match there is between their educational goals and how they handled the tumble of events of the preceding work day.

REFERENCES

Adler, Mortimer. *The Paideia Proposal.* New York: Macmillan, 1982.

Bennett, William. Speech to the National Press Club, 27 March 1985.

Bloom, Benjamin. *Human Characteristics and School Learning.* New York: McGraw-Hill, 1976.

Brameld, Theodore. *Toward a Reconstructed Philosophy of Education.* New York: Dryden Press, 1956.

Buber, Martin. *I and Thou.* Translated by R. G. Smith. 2d ed. New York: Charles Scribner's Sons, 1958.

Ciardi, John. "Informal Remarks to Incoming Freshmen." *Rutgers Alumni Monthly* 34 (November 1954): 2–3.

Counts, George. *Dare the School Build a New Social Order?* New York: John Day, 1932.

Dewey, John. *Democracy and Education.* New York: Macmillan, 1916.

Educational Policy Commission. *The Purposes of Education in American Democracy.* Washington, D.C.: National Education Association, 1938.

Morris, Van Cleve; Crowson, Robert; Hurwitz, Emanuel; and Porter-Gehrie, Cynthia. *Principals in Action: The Reality of Managing Schools.* Columbus, Ohio: Charles E. Merrill Publishing Co., 1984.

Sizer, Theodore. *Horace's Compromise: The Dilemma of the American High School.* Boston: Houghton Mifflin Co., 1984.

Skinner, B. F. *Walden Two.* New York: Macmillan, 1948.

3

School Effectiveness, Backward Mapping, and State Education Policies

Allan Odden

INTRODUCTION

In recent years states have used two strategies to improve the quality of education. One is the creation of broad education reforms that began after the release of *A Nation At Risk* in 1983 by the National Commission on Excellence in Education. This movement was led mainly by state political leaders—governors and legislators. By June 1985 no fewer than twelve states had enacted comprehensive education reform packages funded by large increases in state aid; other states would consider reforms during their 1986 legislative session.

The second strategy is the creation of school improvement programs that began in the late 1970s and early 1980s. This movement was led mainly by state education leaders; it had evolved from years of categorical program administration and increasing state involvement in education policy, and it was often based on the school effectiveness research. By 1982 all states had developed a set of school improvement programs, though they differed in scope, comprehensiveness, and purpose.

Both strategies reflect strong state leadership. They also raise questions. This chapter addresses a number of issues as they relate to these programs. Part one outlines a conceptual framework, called backward mapping, for assessing state and district policy. The premise of backward mapping is that state and district policies should support effective practices in schools and classrooms. Part two presents a summary of the research on classroom and school effectiveness. Part three outlines the state policy implications of that research. Part four discusses state education reforms and school improvement programs in light of the suggested policies outlined in part three and identifies at least one exemplary state program in each policy area. The chapter concludes with comments on how the two strategies reflect the nature of state education politics.

BACKWARD MAPPING

Backward mapping is a bottom-up rather than top-down process for policy development. Typical policy development begins at the top of the system, outlines the policy, and then reasons through various regulations that must be developed to ensure that the policy gets implemented in schools and classrooms. Backward mapping first clarifies the problem, then identifies the service-delivery level where the problem will be addressed directly, then outlines knowledge about effective practices at the service-delivery level, and finally reasons backward (or upward) to identify appropriate policies at each higher level in the system that would support the effective practices at the service-delivery level.

An example of backward mapping might be the following:

1. Stating the problem—poor performance in basic and higher-level thinking skills, for example.
2. Determining where the problem is addressed most directly—as in classrooms and schools.
3. Identifying effective practices at the service-delivery level—from, for example, the research on effective schools, on effective teaching, and on effective principals.
4. Moving up the system to ask how higher levels can help—asking first how school-site administrators can support effective classroom practices.
5. Continuing the process up the policymaking ladder—asking what school districts, intermediate service units, state education agencies, and the political community (governors and

legislators) can do to support effective policies and practices at
´ each level below.

The key to backward mapping for state policymakers is to ask
how they can help sustain effective practices in classrooms and schools,
rather than how they can get state-level policies implemented faith-
fully in local schools. While the idea of backward mapping evolved in
part from a lack of attention to program quality in the administration
of federal and state programs in the 1970s, as a conceptual framework
it can be used to develop public policies in a variety of functional areas
(Elmore 1979–80).

At the same time, faithful implementation of state policy and
development of state policy through the process of backward mapping
are not necessarily in conflict. Backward mapping grew out of the
increasingly narrow and largely fiscal focus of compliance monitoring
for federal and state categorical programs that often ignored issues of
program quality (Elmore and McLaughlin 1982). The thrust of
backward mapping is that effectiveness in classroom and school
practices, not just compliance with administrative rules and regulations, is the prime objective of state and federal programs. Backward
mapping and faithful implementation, thus, can reinforce each other.

RESEARCH ON SCHOOL EFFECTIVENESS

An important step in developing policy by backward mapping is
to identify what is known about effective practices at the service-
delivery level for education, classrooms, and schools. This section
summarizes the research on effective teaching, effective principals,
and effective schools. It also summarizes research on educational
change (specifically for the purpose of school improvement) and state
and federal program implementation. The last two topics are usually
absent from summaries of school effectiveness research, but provide
crucial information on how schools move toward effectiveness.

Effective Teaching

Researchers agree that teachers' *attitudes and expectations* affect their
students' performance. When their attitudes are positive, that is,
when teachers believe students can learn, classroom strategies are

more varied, more homework is assigned and corrected, and students perform better. The students of teachers who approach instruction in a businesslike and task-oriented way achieve at higher levels. Learning is maximized when teachers view academic instruction as basic to their role as teachers, expect students to master the content of the curriculum, and allocate a maximum amount of time to instruction (Good, Biddle, and Brophy 1983).

Classroom management also affects student performance. The more effective teachers maximize the time available for instruction. They are well prepared, maintain a smooth pace during lessons, and do not get confused about what to do next. Transitions between activities are brief and smooth, little time is lost getting organized, and seating configurations, traffic patterns, and material storage are designed to complement instruction. At the beginning of the school year, students are taught the rules governing classroom conduct, use of materials, and classroom procedures.

Teachers' *pedagogical* practices also are important. Active teaching improves student performance, especially for the introduction of new content but also for sequentially ordered content. Active teaching can also be successful for teaching advanced courses to high school and college students (Rosenshine 1983) and higher-level analytic skills (Doyle 1985). Through active teaching, teachers often present information through lecture and demonstration, provide feedback through sequential questions, and prepare students for seatwork that they will successfully complete 80 to 90 percent of. Effective teachers personally convey academic content to students rather than just using curriculum materials. They carefully structure the presentation of content, use advance organizers, set lessons in context, summarize at key points, and review main ideas. They also provide numerous opportunities for practice and feedback by requiring classroom recitation, seatwork, and homework and by sequencing questions from lower to higher levels. Furthermore, effective teachers create a supportive, friendly climate, praise students for specific achievements, turn students' incorrect responses into opportunities for instruction, and focus attention on genuine achievement and mastery (Good 1983).

Appropriate attitudes and expectations, good classroom management, and effective instructional practices combine to maximize "academic learning time," which is the time allocated for instruction during which a student performs successfully. The greater the academic learning time, the greater the achievement (Denham and Lieberman 1980).

Effective Principals

Studies on principals show that their work consists primarily of brief, fragmented, and varied interactions with people. Principals spend 80 percent of their workday in brief encounters with staff, faculty, students, or parents. Desk work takes up only 12 percent of their time, and phone calls 8 percent (Manasse 1985). These work patterns are characteristic of both more and less effective principals.

But in the midst of confusion and competing demands, effective principals use their status and power first to set strategic goals for their schools and then to direct the entire school program toward those goals. Effective principals function as instructional leaders. They enhance effective teaching practices by, for example, assuring more time for instruction and fewer classroom intrusions, assigning students to groups and classrooms to get a pupil mix conducive to high learning, and developing curriculum that is coordinated and articulated across grades and programs. Effective principals create a school climate that supports high expectations for learning, collegial relationships among administrators and faculty, and commitment to continuous improvement. They know the literature on effective teaching and expect teachers to know it. They help teachers use effective teaching strategies in their classrooms and sanction and reward teachers' efforts to improve learning (Manasse 1985).

Effective Schools

In the 1970s several researchers began to report results of studies comparing more effective schools to less effective ones. According to this research, effective schools have five characteristics (Edmonds 1979, 1982): (1) strong instructional leadership by the principal; (2) an academic focus (a coordinated curriculum focused on academic goals and agreement that reaching those goals has priority); (3) teachers who have high expectations that all students can master the curriculum; (4) a system for assessing student performance that is tied to the instructional program and gives teachers information about students' progress; and (5) a climate conducive to learning (safe and orderly, with a discipline code fairly and consistently enforced). Although some researchers questioned the relevance of these findings for secondary schools (Firestone and Herriott 1982), several studies on effective secondary schools have produced similar results (Farrar, Miles, and Neufield 1983; Lightfoot 1983; Lipsitz 1983; and Rutter, Maughan, Mortimore, and Ouston 1979).

In a recent synthesis of research on effective schools, Purkey and Smith (1983) expanded on the characteristics noted by Edmonds to distinguish between organizational and process variables. Fullan (1985), linking these findings with research on educational change, concluded that effective schools have twelve major characteristics:

Organizational
1. Strong instructional leadership, usually but not always from the principal
2. Support from the district office
3. Emphasis on curriculum and instruction
4. Clear goals and high expectations
5. A system to monitor student performance
6. Ongoing staff development, including effective teaching strategies
7. The involvement and support of parents
8. An orderly and secure environment

Process
9. A feel for the change process and the school improvement process on the part of school leaders
10. A value system that directs the schools toward its strategic goals
11. Intense interaction and communication among all people in the school
12. Collaborative planning and implementation of school improvement efforts

Educational Change

Research on educational change suggests that school improvement is a process, not an event. It is a process by which educators alter their ways of thinking and teaching; it is a process of developing new skills and finding them meaningful and satisfying.

Change affects both schools as organizations and the individuals within them (Anderson et al. 1985; Crandall et al. 1983; Louis and Rosenblum 1981). Change can be planned and managed by school and district leaders. In synthesizing a number of studies, Fullan (1985) identifies seven elements of the change process:

1. School improvement takes place over two to three years.
2. The initial stages always produce anxiety and uncertainty (see Hall and Loucks [1982] on stages of concern in the change process).
3. Ongoing assistance and psychological support are crucial to help people cope with anxiety; the assistance must focus on the precise nature of the concern.
4. Change involves learning new skills through practice, feedback, and coaching; change is incremental and developmental.
5. Breakthroughs occur when people understand why a new way works better.
6. Organizational conditions within the school (peer norms and administrative leadership) and outside it (central-office support and external facilitators) make change more or less likely.
7. Successful change requires pressure—specifically, pressure through interaction.

Teachers, principals, central-office staff, and external facilitators usually play different roles in successful school improvement. Teacher commitment, which is critical, comes from mastering new teaching strategies that improve student performance; mastery comes with practice, feedback, and coaching. Teacher commitment does not necessarily come from involvement in determining school goals or strategic directions. Indeed, school improvement is more often successful when administrators exert strong and continuous pressure on teachers to adopt new techniques (Huberman 1983). Although this pressure lowers teacher commitment initially, commitment grows if it is followed by long-term assistance that helps teachers master new practices.

Cox (1983) outlines the roles of principals, central offices, and external facilitators (consultants or staff of state education agencies) in successful school improvement. Generally, principals make sure that all staff know that school improvement is a top priority. They make resources available, give teachers time to practice the techniques in their classrooms, give teachers access to people who can coach them, and allow two to three years for improvement. If principals assist teachers in implementation, they affect teacher outcomes, that is, mastery of practice. If principals focus on schoolwide direction and support, they affect school-level outcomes, that is, schoolwide change and institutionalization. Central-office staff, who usually know the nature of the school, the needs of its students, and the content of the change, are most effective in organizing or conducting training workshops and helping teachers with classroom implementation. Their activities primarily affect individual teachers. Facilitators from outside the district are usually most helpful in preparing a congenial environment for change, that is, ensuring the availability of facilities and resources. When principals, central-office staff, and external facilitators all play key roles, more change takes place and is more successful.

Successful improvement requires that someone provide assistance, mainly to teachers, focused on the *content* of change, that is, someone should help teachers implement new practices (Joyce and Showers 1982). It also requires that someone provide assistance focused on the *context* of change, that is, get approvals, resources, and facilities (Cox 1983). Anyone can play these roles, but the research suggests that the divisions of labor described above tend to dominate.

In short, many mysteries of educational change have been solved. Moreover, most successful improvement is engineered, it does not just happen. Successful improvement is the result of leadership and planned action.

State and Federal Program Implementation

Research findings on program implementation complement findings on educational change. Successful implementation takes time, is more effective if it is integrated rather than maintained as a separate program, and must include ongoing technical assistance (coaching). Federal and state compensatory, bilingual, vocational, and special education programs have increased financial resources, expanded educational services, and created state and district capacity to develop and implement programs.

Early studies of federal and state program implementation showed how rules and regulations (compliance and monitoring activities) increased at the expense of technical assistance, the key element in the change process. The evolution of the Elementary and Secondary Education Act of 1965 (now the Education Consolidation and' Improvement Act of 1982) is a good example. The original bill included Title I, which provided substantial new funds for services to low-income, educationally disadvantaged children, plus other titles that provided money for the development of pilot programs, practical research, and technical assistance. The intent was to allow local districts flexibility to design programs to fit their needs and to help them implement these programs (Elmore and McLaughlin 1982). But interest in assistance gradually eroded and regulations grew. Federal practice fostered state practices that also emphasized compliance and coercion, and many states began to see regulation as the best vehicle for education reform (Murphy 1982).

In the late 1970s practices began to change. Research on the implementation of federal school improvement programs began to show that providing technical assistance to schools and districts could improve education. Drawing on this work and the research on school effectiveness, states began a wide range of school improvement, technical assistance programs (McLaughlin 1983).

The Symbolic Elements of School Improvement

The technical and educational components of school improvement are well known. But successful school improvement is not just a technical activity. It must be guided by a skilled leader who has technical knowledge as well as a feel for the change process. Such a leader must fuse the technology of school effectiveness with a school culture that sustains hard work, builds collegial interaction, and maintains trust and respect. Good teaching and learning require commitment and engagement (Cohen 1983), and successful school improvement requires time and energy (Anderson et al. 1985). To develop commitment and to release energy, effective school leaders manipulate symbols to control and direct behavior.

Good principals manage symbols effectively. They centralize the school on key values and decentralize all else. They outline their vision of the school to everyone in the school, then manage the goal-setting activities to implement the vision. They generate commitment to these goals. They announce expectations for students and teachers, and they model norms. They use rituals, symbols, and slogans to hold things together. Capitalizing on their fragmented work patterns, they spend considerable time reminding people of their vision. They monitor progress toward goals and teach people to interpret efforts and progress in a common language. They reward teachers who improve, and they protect teachers who attempt innovation (Manasse 1984). Their style of leadership is similar to effective leadership in the private sector (Kotter 1982).

Essential to symbolic leadership is a compelling vision. The vision is the substance of what is communicated through symbolic actions. The symbolic actions, in turn, help build the culture that bonds students, teachers, and others in the work of that school (Sergiovanni 1984). Symbolic leaders articulate school purpose and mission; socialize members into the school culture; tell stories, myths, and legends to maintain and reinforce traditions; explain the "way things happen here"; and reward people for fitting into the culture. The culture identifies what is of worth in a school and governs how people should feel and behave. Successful schools have strong cultures that steer people in a common direction. Strong cultures, moreover, are created, that is, they are nurtured and built by school leaders. They are what tightly couples effective schools.

IMPLICATIONS FOR STATE POLICY

States cannot mandate effective schools: the essence of an effective school is a strong culture, which derives from a strategic independence. Yet, states can help create and sustain school effectiveness in at least seven ways: (1) providing symbolic leadership to raise the status of education; (2) articulating clear state educational goals; (3) building awareness of the school effectiveness research; (4) developing system incentives that recognize and reward school effectiveness; (5) providing technical assistance to schools; (6) altering training and certification requirements; and (7) strengthening state data gathering.

Symbolic Leadership

Symbolic leadership at the state level helps place education on the policy agenda. The national reports of 1983 and the various state task forces, together with strong gubernatorial leadership in most states, are probably why education became a priority issue in the states in 1984. In addition, reports from national and state task forces can produce symbols of concensus about what to improve in education.

Symbolic leadership can also raise the status of education. Governors and business leaders view improved public education as essential to revitalizing the country's economy and sustaining national economic growth. Both the status of the people making these claims and the claims themselves help give political prominence to education.

State leaders can use new metaphors to describe education and the work of the people in it. Schools could be described as "knowledge work organizations," teachers as "managers of knowledge workers," and principals as "managers of knowledge work managers" (Schlechty and Joslin 1984). Teaching can be described as a set of executive functions: planning; communicating goals; regulating activities in the workplace; educating new members of the work group; and supervising, motivating, and evaluating other people (Berliner 1983). Education could be described as the central activity of the information, high-technology society and as critical to the development of human capital. By using metaphors that project symbols the country values, state leaders could help solidify a new stature for education.

State leaders can also establish mechanisms for celebrating excellence in education, like annual award dinners for outstanding teachers, recognition days for exemplary schools, governors' awards for education improvement, legislative scholar awards, and travel grants for outstanding teachers and principals. The U.S. Secretary of Education recognized 150 exemplary secondary schools in 1983 and 200 in 1984, recognized local school boards that created vibrant education reform programs in 1984, and established student reward programs. Similar programs could be developed in each of the fifty states. Such programs and ceremonies keep the symbols of educational excellence in public view.

Articulating Goals

Generally, states have not clearly articulated the academic goals of education. Mission statements are often diffuse; Goodlad (1983) found that academic goals are not primary in most states. Lack of clarity does not help districts or schools focus their energies. A statement of academic goals is one of the hallmarks of effective schools. The national reports generally concur that academic goals ought to be reemphasized, and largely represent a consensus on what they ought to be. The time may be ripe for states to set clear academic goals and stipulate that attaining those goals is the primary purpose of the education system. Following the findings on effective schools, academic goals could include, as a floor, acceptable performance in the basic skills of reading, writing, and mathematics; for secondary students, academic goals could cut across the various subject areas by emphasizing higher-level thinking skills such as probem solving, analyzing, drawing conclusions, synthesizing, writing persuasive arguments, and transferring knowledge to new contexts. This cross subject-department focus might help high schools create schoolwide cultures that could bind them together.

Awareness of Research

There is a lag between the emergence of new research results, their dissemination, and their use in new teaching strategies. States could develop and disseminate information on school effectiveness to educators by writing newsletters, holding seminars, and sponsoring conferences for teachers, administrators, and staff and by developing state diffusion networks, similar to the national diffusion network, to encourage people in different districts to share knowledge with one another.

System Incentives

Effective principals reward teachers and students for meeting key goals. Using monetary and nonmonetary rewards, the culture of effective schools positively reinforces in formal and informal ways those who embody its values. Yet state and local public education systems often have few "system incentives" or formal mechanisms to recognize and reward outstanding performance by teachers, administrators, schools, or students; nor do they provide "loose" funds at the building level for discretionary use by the principal. At modest cost, states could give districts and schools incentives to meet key state goals by providing the following:

— Planning grants. One way principals produce consensus on school goals is through the planning process. Yet, few districts and schools now have planning funds.
— Productivity bonuses for districts or schools that meet improvement or productivity goals. States could fiscally reward schools that meet or move toward key state goals.
— Competitive grants to administrators and teachers, like the old federal Title IV-C, for the development of innovative programs and materials.
— Pay-for-performance systems for compensating teachers, like career ladder, master teacher, or mentor programs, or annual bonuses for outstanding teachers. Pay structures for teachers could be altered to target new responsibilities and economic rewards to teachers who perform at the highest levels on the key goals and objectives of the state, district, and school.
— School-site budgeting. Research shows that improvement occurs school by school. Thus, increasing the scope of school-site budgeting may be in order. The strategic independence needed by effective schools includes resource independence as well. Principals need more control over resources to manage them effectively.

Technical Assistance Programs

Research on school effectiveness, especially research on program implementation, suggests strongly that a shift in strategy from regulation to technical assistance is needed to improve the quality of local programs. Further, research suggests also a shift from district to school programs. One example of a technical assistance strategy is the state-run *effective schools programs*, in which schools participate voluntarily and staff of the state education agency help them to assess the degree to which they have the characteristics of effective schools, to design programs to develop those characteristics, and to implement the programs. Another example is state *school improvement programs* that provide more generalized technical assistance. A third example is *instructional alignment programs*, which draw on an important subcomponent of effective schools. State agency staff could help districts align academic goals, instructional materials, and tests.

Training and Certification

The most obvious use of the research on effective teaching and principals is to incorporate it into in-service and preservice training. States could require that the research and validated training programs based on it be included in teacher-preparation programs. Further, the state could develop *in-service-training programs in instructional effectiveness* in which state-agency staff or consultants could train teachers in the field. States could also develop new models for coordinating the training at teacher-training institutions with training and support programs in school districts, especially for beginning teachers. In this way, professors, student teachers, and supervising teachers could share a common perspective and a common language.

In addition, states could use school effectiveness research for in-service-training programs for administrators and academies for principals. Now that the research has become clearer, these programs could focus on the skills and techniques required for building-level instructional leadership.

Finally, states could alter their criteria for selecting and certifying principals. Principals need to know about effective teaching, know how to observe it in classrooms, be skilled at clinical supervision, know how to develop an integrated schoolwide curriculum, understand the technical and interpersonal components of the change literature, and judge the effect of management and administrative decisions on the instructional program. These are the kinds of competencies that need to be included in certification requirements. These competencies should dominate selection criteria but usually do not (Baltzell and Dentler 1983).

State Data Gathering

Over the past ten years states have expanded programs to test students and teachers. But few, if any, states have developed testing programs to show how the state education system is doing over time on key state goals.

As a beginning, states could develop instruments that could be used to provide indicators of effective schools and districts. Districts generally cannot afford to create instruments that are research based, valid, and useful for school planning. Also, states could actually gather and disseminate data on school and district effectiveness as a way of broadcasting excellence and pressuring less effective schools to do better. Indicators of school effectiveness are not limited to test scores.

States could also expand the formative monitoring of school improvement programs or education reform programs to identify problems, document obstacles, outline new ways to proceed, and describe impacts. The result of this monitoring could be supplied directly to technical assistance units that would help districts and schools work out implementation problems.

Finally, states could reconstitute student-testing programs to provide information on the status of and change over time in student achievement. For state-policy purposes, these programs would not—nor should not—test all students, either in any subject or in any grade. Universal individual testing is the responsibility of the teacher, school, and district. State policymakers need information on how the state's education *system* is functioning; this information can be provided efficiently through matrix sampling techniques that have been refined by the National Assessment of Educational Progress (NAEP) over the past fifteen years. Indeed, states could piggyback on NAEP testing and, over time, produce useful information on performance in basic skills, critical subject areas, and higher-level thinking skills at a cost below what some are now spending. The results could be used to assess strengths and weaknesses in the state system. The results could also be used to compare the state's results to the regional or national results reported by NAEP.

STATE PROGRAMS ON SCHOOL EFFECTIVENESS: THEIR RELATIONSHIP TO POLICIES IMPLIED BY SCHOOL EFFECTIVENESS RESEARCH

How do current policies for school effectiveness measure up to the policies suggested by the school effectiveness research? This section first discusses the degree to which programs of school improvement and of education reform match the suggested policies in the previous section and then identifies exemplary state programs in each of seven areas of state policy.

State School Improvement Programs

A fifty-state survey conducted by the Education Commission of the States in 1982 identified a range of programs that had been developed by state education agencies over a five-year period (Odden and Dougherty 1982). The programs emphasized technical assistance, were school based, and were often based on the school effectiveness research. They included new state dissemination programs, a number of system incentives, numerous technical assistance programs, altered certification requirements, new state in-service training initiatives, and revised state data gathering. The programs, though varying in focus and scope, are now well spread: thirty-seven states have school or district planning requirements, fifteen have effective schools projects, forty-four have state-run staff-development programs for teachers and thirty-one have them for administrators, twenty-nine states have incentive programs for teachers, and sixteen have new intern-year programs for beginning teachers.

In general, these programs are consonant with the policy implications of the school effectiveness research. Preliminary analysis indicates that they reflect a change in the behavior of state education agencies from regulation to technical assistance, spring from leadership within the education community (often the state's chief school officer), and emanate largely from the school effectiveness research (including some research on change), but are funded at a relatively low level with categorical funds that can easily disappear (Burnes, Fuhrman, Odden, and Palaich 1983). Evaluative research on their impacts is generally positive, and research across states shows that state initiative and leadership can be vital to successful implementation of local school improvement activities (Anderson et al. 1985).

State Education Reform Programs

A study of education reform programs in eight states found that they appear to overlook technical assistance and emphasize the hardware of education excellence—higher expectations, tougher standards, stiffer requirements, and better curriculum (Odden 1984).

Stiffer standards across the board and a school finance reform were critical in Arkansas. Greater high school course requirements and the addition of a seventh period in high school were key components in Florida. Reinstatement of minimum high school graduation require-ments and tougher courses were important in California. A high school exit examination and merit pay were pivotal in South Carolina. Expanded student testing and grade-to-grade promotion were empha-sized in Texas. A career ladder structure for teacher compensation was the cornerstone of Tennessee's reform.

In addition, these eight states revised and strengthened school finance formulas; increased funding for special education, compensa-tory, and bilingual programs; and allocated most new dollars through fiscal equalization programs, thus reinforcing equity programs of the 1970s.

Upon closer examination, it turns out that most state education reform programs also expanded and strengthened school improve-ment initiatives. Arkansas increased staff in the state education agency by almost 33 percent to help implement its new educational standards and also to expand training in instructional leadership, effective teaching, classroom management, and effective schools. Cal-ifornia established centers for in-service training of teachers and widened its large school improvement program. South Carolina started a new teaching program based on the Arkansas Program of Effective Teaching (PET), expanded its administrator academy, and funded a state assessment center for principals. Texas strengthened the capacity of its state education department to provide technical assistance, and Utah put funds into a productivity program.

While the expansion of school improvement initiatives occurred as part of many education reforms, the connection between them may be more a matter of accident than of design. South Carolina, however, consciously fused the two and created an education reform implemen-tation unit as a temporary project in the state education agency. About fifteen new staff members help local districts and schools carry out education reform programs. The unit's mission is to identify problems, document obstacles, help local educators work out im-plementation bugs, and report annually to the governor and legis-lature on the progress of implementation. In creating the unit, legislators recognized specifically that the new education reform programs were major programmatic thrusts that required additional state technical assistance if local districts were to implement them successfully.

Exemplary State Programs Supporting School Effectiveness

While state action in school improvement and education reform reflects at least in spirit the thrust of policies suggested by backward mapping, few states include all the programs suggested by backward mapping even if their school improvement and education reform programs are combined. To outline what a comprehensive set of such programs might be, this section identifies at least one exemplary state program in each of the seven policy areas outlined by backward mapping.

Symbolic Leadership

State leaders, especially governors, have provided the type of symbolic leadership needed to place education high on state policy agendas. Governors James Hunt of North Carolina, Lamar Alexander of Tennessee, Bill Clinton of Arkansas, Richard Riley of South Carolina, and Mark White of Texas, for example, literally spent the bulk of their time over a six- to eighteen-month period putting education reform on the top of the policy agenda and moving education reform packages through the legislative process. The more than 250 state education commissions and task forces have helped develop symbolic consensus about what needs to be reformed in each state. The new language is upbeat and positive, which is a change from just a few years ago; the purpose is to produce quality, not just root out incompetence. At the symbolic level of focusing public attention on the problem and catalyzing political action, state political and educational leaders have performed well.

Setting State Education Goals

States have taken important but incomplete steps in setting academic goals. Perhaps the most lasting accomplishment in this arena will be the new climate states have developed for education systems. Nearly all states have raised academic expectations for children, and nearly all have raised high school graduation requirements. About 50 percent have raised college admission requirements, nearly all are tightening educational standards generally, and most are strengthening the curriculum. These contributions to fostering a school climate that supports higher achievement are important.

More-specific action on specifying academic goals, however, is harder to identify. States that have developed new mission statements identify the purposes of the education system mainly as modern statements of the seven cardinal principles. The most specific identification of academic goals occurs in those states with new or expanded testing programs, but the focus primarily is on the basic skills of reading, writing, and mathematics; occasionally these are expanded to include communication and science. No state has made acquisition of a range of higher-level analytic and thinking skills the key academic objective of the education system. Making the tough decisions on the key purposes of the education system is probably a major unfinished piece of business in most states. Effective schools, it seems, identify their academic goals and pursue them vigorously; to help foster effectiveness in all schools, most states need to specify more clearly the academic goals of the state's education system.

Building an Awareness of Research

Arkansas and Minnesota have created state diffusion networks to spread the news about effective programs and policies. Particular attention is given to effective practices developed by districts within each state, including a focus on effective rural programs in Arkansas.

System Incentives

In the past five years states have enacted a variety of incentive programs designed to spur initiative for the purpose of school improvement.

Planning Grants. California's School Improvement Program (SIP) exemplifies the oldest and most generous program of planning grants. Now in its twelfth year, SIP provides $30 per student to local schools for developing a school improvement program. The planning grants must be used to create a school-site education improvement council, to assess strengths and weaknesses of the school, and to develop a long-term plan to improve the weak areas. Implementation grants, now at about $106 per student, are provided for a three-year period and are renewable if implementation is successful. The state is striving to provide school improvement operation grants to all schools in the state. Research has shown this approach to be relatively successful (Berman and Gjelten 1984; Odden 1985).

Productivity Bonuses. The idea of recognizing and rewarding schools that improve on the key goals of a state has caught on in a few states. Florida has a $20 million program for merit schools, and South Carolina has a $28 million program to reward school productivity. In South Carolina, schools will be eligible for an extra $7 per pupil for improvement or performance at a high absolute level on up to four of a variety of factors. Improved academic achievement, community satisfaction, lower dropout rates, and reduced teacher or student absenteeism are examples of some factors. As the program is phased in over a three-year period, the per-pupil dollars in the state's new remedial program will be reduced slightly. The productivity program, thus, serves as a mechanism to reward schools successful in remedial efforts.

Competitive Grants for Teachers and Administrators. Arkansas, California, and South Carolina included minigrant programs in their education reform programs that give teachers small grants, such as $2,000 to develop innovative programs or materials. In West Virginia the business community funded a state education foundation for the purpose of providing such grants to talented and creative teachers.

Pay-for-Performance Systems. Many states have developed variations of pay-for-performance plans. Tennessee designed the most comprehensive state plan. Its career ladder plan, designed to restructure the compensation system for teachers, has five rungs: (1) probationary teacher, with a one-year term preceding either promotion to the second rung or dismissal; (2) apprentice teacher, with a one-year term and $500 salary supplement, followed by promotion or dismissal; (3) career level I, with a five-year renewable term and a $1,000 salary supplement; (4) career level II, with a five-year renewable term and a $2,000 or $4,000 salary supplement for a 10- or 11-month contract; and (5) career level III, with a five-year renewable term and a $3,000,

$5,000, or $7,000 salary supplement for a 10-, 11-, or 12-month contract. Participation in the Tennessee plan is voluntary, but the plan is the same for all districts. Other states have provided seed money for districts to develop local plans; the long-term funding and impact of these approaches need to be analyzed in the future.

Already, the program in Utah has produced encouraging results. School districts receive $200 per pupil to support locally designed career ladder programs. Most districts have used the funds to compensate teachers for additional work, usually work that engages teachers in schoolwide activities such as planning, developing school improvement programs, creating new curriculum, and training new teachers or in providing in-service training for experienced teachers. Teachers view more pay for more work as a legitimate reason for differentiated compensation. By structuring the new jobs as schoolwide activities, the program has helped to improve collegiality and to develop a schoolwide culture of continuous improvement, key characteristics of effective schools. Thus, the structure of career ladder programs can fulfill a dual role: providing promotional opportunities for teachers and stimulating effective school climates.

School-Site Budgeting. No state has developed programs to stimulate school-site budgeting or outcomes-based budgeting at the building level as part of either school improvement programs or education reform programs. While California and Florida initiated such plans in the 1970s as part of school finance reforms, there has been relatively little discussion of whether policies for resource allocation and use need adjustment as a result of targeting the school as the unit for education improvement. Yet, sound mechanisms for outcomes-based budgeting at the school level are working successfully in some local districts (Bailey 1983).

Technical Assistance

As stated previously, expansion of state technical assistance activities to improve local program quality is one of the clearest hallmarks of state initiatives in the past five to seven years. Many state education leaders have read the research that identifies long-term coaching and supportive help as key to school improvement and know that states must add technical assistance activities to their traditional compliance and regulatory responsibilities.

Effective Schools Projects. Connecticut developed what is now the most senior but constantly changing effective schools project. Schools participate voluntarily, and state education agency staff help schools (1) assess the degree to which they have the characteristics of effective schools; (2) design programs to develop those characteristics; and (3) implement the programs. Their instrument for assessing the characteristics of effective schools is used by many schools and districts across the country.

School Improvement Projects. Colorado's "clusters" program is an example of a more generalized school improvement strategy. Each cluster of schools works on a different component of school improvement—school climate, effective teaching, effective school characteristics—and each is assisted by staff from the state education agency and the regional service unit. Maryland's school improvement program includes teacher training in one of four instructional models of effective teaching and a small grant to implement the program locally. As mentioned previously, California provides grants of about $106 per student for schools to implement school improvement plans; the funds are increasingly being used to purchase the supports (trainers, consultants, materials, and so forth) needed to undergird a change process.

Training and Certification

One of the most comprehensive state *in-service* training programs is the Arkansas Program for Effective Teaching (PET). Now in its sixth year, PET draws on mastery learning, Madeline Hunter's program of clinical teaching, and research on effective teaching. It includes a twenty-five-day cycle of presentation, classroom practice, observation, and feedback. The state's program objectives are (1) to train PET instructors who then train teachers in local training cycles and (2) to develop clinical supervision skills for principals and others who supervise teachers. The state's goal is to improve student performance in the basic skills.

Preservice training has been less affected by the knowledge from research on effective teaching. In Arkansas, though, nearly half the professors in teacher-training institutions have been trained in PET techniques. As a result, the link between university programs, supervising teachers, and student teachers has been strengthened.

Induction programs or beginning teacher programs have been developed in Georgia, Oklahoma, Pennsylvania, and South Carolina. The objective in all four programs is to provide beginning teachers more assistance in their first year to help them transfer skills to the classroom. Licenses are not provided until the first year is completed successfully.

In-service programs for principals have emerged in many states; those in Arkansas, Florida, South Carolina, and North Carolina are the most developed. Arkansas has moved its administrators' academy into training in instructional management skills, in addition to the PET program's focus on clinical supervision. South Carolina has funded a state center for the assessment of principals, patterned after the assessment center developed by the National Association of Secondary School Principals, as a way to screen new principals. The program assesses each individual's expertise in a number of skill areas and identifies areas in which additional training is needed.

A study by the Education Commission of the States investigated the implementation and impact of new state technical assistance and training programs in ten states and forty schools and found numerous examples of successful impact at the local level. The study confirmed a clear and strong role for the state in supporting local strategies for school improvement (Anderson et al. 1985).

State Data Gathering

Most state activity has moved in the direction of collecting test data from all students in order to measure performance in basic skills at different grade levels. There is scant discussion of clear state academic goals and development of specific indicators to show how the state is progressing over time. There is beginning to be discussion of the need for data to describe how a state's education system is progressing statewide (including discussion at the federal level to provide such information for all fifty states). The California Indicators of Quality is conceptualized to provide this information; release of the first round of indicators occurred in mid 1985. The Policy

Analysis for California Education (PACE) project at Stanford University, the University of California at Berkeley, and the University of Southern California produces an annual document that outlines the condition of education in California and the changes in education over time.

Colorado has developed two instruments related to effective schools—"Indicators of Quality Schools" and "Indicators of Quality School Districts"—that draw on school effectiveness research and can be administered in local districts and schools. Ohio has developed eight indicators of success to monitor district progress in the state school improvement–effective schools program.

Summary

While there are exemplary state programs in each of the seven areas of policy suggested by backward mapping from the school effectiveness research, it would be difficult to identify any state that has developed policies in all seven areas. The PET program in Arkansas is an example of an integrated set of activities focused on developing effective teaching; even here, additional policies such as changing state certification requirements could be implemented to ensure that the program has a wider impact. While California's SIP program is a good example of a program designed to produce a capacity for change in local schools, recent evaluation has shown that unless the content of change is specified, it is difficult to determine the combined impact of the effort; California is moving both to define the content of change (curriculum improvement) and to make the program available to all schools. Finally, many of even the best state initiatives struggle on unstable, and low-level, categorical funding. Unless states commit serious levels of resources to such programs over a long time period, like California has done for SIP, it would be difficult for any of them individually or in combination to reflect a comprehensive and integrated response to the implications of the school effectiveness research.

CONCLUSION

The strength of the backward-mapping approach to education policy development is its focus on first identifying effective practices at the service-delivery level (classrooms and schools) and then identifying policies that can be adopted by higher levels of government to support those practices. It seeks to ensure that higher-level policies affect the problem being addressed, rather than veer off the mark over time and focus on indirect issues such as fiscal tracking. Backward mapping, however, does not deal directly with the broader issues of politics and finance, both of which are important components of policy development in any state.

For example, the development of state school improvement programs was a movement from within the education community reflecting a backward-mapping approach. Such programs represented new directions for state education agencies and significant change for state education leaders. But initially they lacked either sanction by or political support from the state's general political leaders—governors and legislators. They were virtually unrecognized by any of the national education reports or by reports from state task forces. They were weakly funded and were the target of funding cuts when funds decreased. As McDonnell and McLaughlin (1982) suggest, significant new directions in state education policy need the support of general political actors in order to succeed. Thus, school improvement reflects backward mapping but has little chance of succeeding unless it gains political recognition, support, and stable funding. The Education Commission of the State's study of state strategies that support local school improvement reached the same conclusion (Anderson et al. 1985).

Arkansas provides an example. A new chief school officer at the state level began a series of school improvement initiatives in 1979 that represented significant divergence from the previous behavior of the state department. Though identified as creative new state leadership (Odden 1983), the programs were underfunded with small amounts of federal funds. Not until the legislature and governor became convinced that the programs could be used to implement the education reform package enacted in 1983 did the programs receive recognition, sanction, and stable state funding.

Education reforms, by contrast, were the products of state political leaders. Governors, legislators, and business leaders—not educators—created these programs that were unabashedly designed to reform the state education system. Also, they were funded with large infusions of new state dollars (Odden 1984). Though designed to improve quality, education reform programs fell short of those suggested by backward mapping and focused more on higher standards, longer days, stiffer requirements, and pay for teachers.

These two movements, thus, provide lessons about the inextricable links between education and politics. Political leaders put issues on the agenda, sanction change, and provide new levels of funds. That requires tough action in complex political arenas. The accompanying rhetoric is strong. Subtleties are ignored.

Education leaders, by contrast, have difficulty setting new strategic directions on their own, at least at the state level. School improvement, which languished for years, only now is solidifying in some states, mainly because it is seen as the means for implementing politically designed education reforms, not because it reflects so well backward mapping from school effectiveness research.

Further, in assessing the relationship between the policies implied by backward mapping and those in education reforms, one must recognize that the latter may include objectives not included in backward mapping from school effectiveness research. Many elements in state education reforms are targeted as a group on improving the quality of people entering and remaining in the teaching profession. While such a policy focus should reinforce school effectiveness over time, it is a different policy focus and, as such, is difficult to assess from a backward-mapping perspective.

Finally, and returning to a theme discussed at the beginning of this chapter, backward mapping is one approach to the development of education policy that should not exclude strategies implied by other approaches. Mandates and regulatory provisions still have their place. Indeed, even incentive mechanisms may not change the behavior of all people, schools, or districts. The genius of backward mapping is that it shows how policy can be developed from the bottom up as well as from the top down, and that technical assistance and incentives are powerful tools that historically have been underused, but which can be used quite successfully in state education programs (Anderson et al. 1985).

REFERENCES

Anderson, Beverly; Odden, Allan; Farrar, Eleanor; Fuhrman, Susan; Davis, Alan; Huddle, Gene; Armstrong, Jane; and Flakus-Mosqueda, Patty. *State Strategies to Support Local School Improvement*. Denver: Education Commission of the States, 1985.

Bailey, George. "Focusing Local Resources on School Improvement." In *School Finance and School Improvement: Linkages for the 1980s*, edited by Allan Odden and L. Dean Webb. Cambridge, Mass.: Ballinger, 1983.

Baltzell, D. Catherine, and Dentler, Robert A. *Selecting American School Principals: A Sourcebook for Educators*. Washington, D.C.: National Institute of Education, 1983.

Berliner, David. "If Teachers Were Thought of as Executives: Implications for Teacher Preparation and Certification." Paper prepared for the National Institute of Education, 1983.

Berman, Paul, and Gjelten, Tom. *Improving School Improvement*. Vol. 2. Berkeley, Calif.: Berman, Weiler Associates, 1984.

Burnes, Donald W.; Fuhrman, Susan; Odden, Allan; and Palaich, Robert. "State-Initiated School Improvement: A Study of Four States." Denver: Education Commission of the States, 1983.

Cohen, Michael. "Instructional, Management, and Social Conditions in Effective Schools." In *School Finance and School Improvement: Linkages for the 1980s*, edited by Allan Odden and L. Dean Webb. Cambridge, Mass.: Ballinger, 1983.

Cox, Pat L. "Complementary Roles in Successful Change." *Educational Leadership* 41 (November 1983): 10–13.

Crandall, David, and associates. *People, Policies, and Practices: Examining the Chain of School Improvement*. Andover, Mass.: The Network, 1983.

Denham, Carolyn, and Lieberman, Ann, eds. *A Time to Learn*. Washington, D.C.: National Institute of Education, 1980.

Doyle, Walter. "Effective Classroom Practices (Secondary)." In *Effective Schools Sourcebook*. Washington, D.C.: National Institute of Education, 1985.

Edmonds, Ronald. "Effective Schools for the Urban Poor." *Educational Leadership* 37 (October 1979): 15–27.

Edmonds, Ronald. "Programs of School Improvement." *Educational Leadership* 40 (December 1982): 4–11.

Elmore, Richard. "Backward Mapping: Implementation Research and Policy Decisions." *Political Science Quarterly* 94 (Winter 1979–80): 601–616.

Elmore, Richard, and McLaughlin, Milbrey. "Strategic Choice in Federal Education Policy: The Compliance-Assistance Trade-off." In *Policy Making in Education*, Eighty-first Yearbook of the National Society for the Study of Education, Part 1, edited by Ann Lieberman and Milbrey McLaughlin. Chicago: University of Chicago Press, 1982.

Farrar, Eleanor; Miles, Matthew B.; and Neufeld, Barbara. "A Review of Effective Schools Research: The Message for Secondary Schools." Paper prepared for the

National Commission of Excellence in Education. Cambridge, Mass.: Huron Institute, 1983.

Firestone, William A., and Herriott, Robert E. "Prescriptions for Effective Elementary Schools Don't Fit Secondary Schools." *Educational Leadership* 40 (December 1982): 51–53.

Fullan, Michael. "Change Processes and Strategies at the Local Level." *Elementary School Journal* 85 (January 1985): 391-421.

Good, Thomas. "Research on Classroom Teaching." In *Handbook of Teaching and Policy* edited by Lee S. Shulman and Gary Sykes. New York: Longman, 1983.

Good, Thomas; Biddle, Bruce J.; and Brophy, Jere E. "Teaching Effectiveness: Research Findings and Policy Implications." Paper prepared for the National Institute of Education, 1983.

Goodlad, John. *A Place Called School.* New York: McGraw-Hill, 1983.

Hall, Gene E. and Loucks, Susan F. "Bridging the Gap: Policy Research Rooted in Practice." In *Policy Making in Education*, Eighty-first Yearbook of the National Society for the Study of Education, Part I, edited by Ann Lieberman and Milbrey McLaughlin. Chicago: University of Chicago Press, 1982.

Huberman, A. Michael. "School Improvement Strategies That Work: Some Scenarios." *Educational Leadership* 41 (November 1983): 23–27.

Joyce, Bruce, and Showers, Beverly. "Coaching of Teaching." *Educational Leadership* 40 (October 1982): 4–8.

Kotter, John P. "What Effective General Managers Do." *Harvard Business Review* 60 (November-December 1982):

Lightfoot, Sara Lawrence. *The Good High School: Portraits of Character and Culture.* New York: Basic Books, 1983.

Lipsitz, Joan. *Successful Schools for Young Adolescents.* Chapel Hill: University of North Carolina, 1983.

Louis, Karen S., and Rosenblum, Sheila. *Strategies for Knowledge Use and School Improvement.* Washington, D. C.: National Institute of Education, 1981.

McDonnell, Lorraine, and McLaughlin, Milbrey. *Education Policy and the Role of the States.* Santa Monica, Calif.: Rand Corporation, 1982.

McLaughlin, Milbrey W. "State Involvement in Local Education Quality." In *School Finance and School Improvement: Linkages for the 1980s*, edited by Allan Odden and L. Dean Webb. Cambridge, Mass.: Ballinger, 1983.

Manasse, A. Lorri. "Principals as Leaders in High-Performing Systems." *Educational Leadership* 41 (February 1984): 42–46.

Manasse, A. Lorri. "Improving Conditions for Principal Effectiveness: Policy Implications of Research." *Elementary School Journal* 85 (January 1985): 439–463.

Murphy, Jerome T. "Progress and Problems: The Paradox of State Reform." In *Policy Making in Education*, Eighty-first Yearbook of the National Society for the Study of Education, Part 1, edited by Ann Lieberman and Milbrey McLaughlin. Chicago: University of Chicago Press, 1982.

National Commission on Excellence in Education. *A Nation At Risk: The Imperative for Educational Reform.* Washington, D.C.: U.S. Government Printing Office, 1983.

Odden, Allan. "School Improvement in Arkansas." Denver: Education Commission of the States, 1983.

Odden, Allan. *Education Finance in the States: 1984.* Denver: Education Commission of the States, 1984.

Odden, Allan. "California Local Analytic Memorandum." Denver: Education Commission of the States, 1985.

Odden, Allan, and Dougherty, Van. *State Programs of School Improvement: A Fifty State Survey.* Denver: Education Commission of the States, 1982.

Purkey, Stewart C., and Smith, Marshall S. "Effective Schools: A Review." *Elementary School Journal* 83 (March 1983) 427–452.

Rosenshine, Barak. "Teaching Functions in Instructional Programs." *Elementary School Journal* 83 (March 1983): 335–351.

Rutter, Michael; Maughan, Barbara; Mortimore, Peter; and Ouston, Janet. *Fifteen Thousand Hours: Secondary Schools and Their Effects on Children.* Cambridge, Mass.: Harvard University Press, 1979.

Schlechty, Phillip C., and Joslin, Anne Walker. "Images of Schools." *Teachers College Record* 86 (Fall 1984): 156–170.

Sergiovanni, Thomas J. "Leadership and Excellence in Schooling." *Educational Leadership* 41 (February 1984): 4–13.

II

Research on
Educational Effects

4

Successful Implementation of Instruction at Inner-City Schools

Daniel U. Levine, Rayna F. Levine, and Eugene E. Eubanks

Our purpose in this chapter is to provide a research-based commentary that summarizes generalizations that can be made regarding instruction-related practices and policies and their implementation at effective inner-city schools. We define effective inner-city schools as schools with a high proportion of poverty students whose academic achievement (usually defined by reading scores) is considerably higher than similar poverty schools. This discussion focuses on inner-city elementary schools, but most of the generalizations we discuss can be applied at inner-city secondary schools and, probably, at mixed-class schools as well. The generalizations we discuss will center on the following interrelated topics and themes: outcomes-based instruction; effective organizational arrangements for low achievers; coordination of instruction; avoidance of pitfalls and dangers, particularly those that involve overemphasis on lower-order skills; "operationalization" of shared values; organic implementation; and selection of overall instructional approach.

GENERALIZATIONS

1. *Instruction at effective inner-city schools is outcomes-based.* It is critically important to devise and implement an outcomes-based instruc-

Reprinted, with permission, from *Journal of Negro Education* 54 (1985): 313–332.

tional system at inner-city schools. If only because many students in these schools are performing far below grade level, teachers cannot allow instruction to drift too much away from the most important learning outcomes. Emphasis on key objectives also is required to facilitate unified efforts on the part of teachers, administrators, students, parents, and others involved in the total school enterprise.

In our view there are two major, interrelated strands involved in conceptualizing and implementing an outcomes-based instructional system. The first is the concept and practice of *curriculum alignment*; the second is *mastery learning* of one kind or another. In practice, curriculum alignment and mastery learning are virtually inseparable because they both involve planning and delivery of instruction to ensure that students acquire important learning skills.

In a general sense, *curriculum alignment* refers to the coordination of learning objectives, instructional materials and methods, and assessments (including tests) of students' progress and learning problems so that the instructional program is consistent in delivering instruction that focuses on the most important learning outcomes. Successful approaches to curriculum alignment have been described in several studies of effective inner-city schools. In general, these approaches either provide for staff development in which faculties identify and select appropriate teaching objectives, materials, and methods in accordance with data on their students' learning needs, as in the Los Angeles Curriculum Alignment Project (Niedermeyer and Yelon 1981), or they emphasize internally aligned materials, as in the Chicago Mastery Learning Reading Program (Levine and Stark 1982).

Mastery learning can refer either to general *mastery-based* programs or to full-fledged *corrective mastery learning* of the kind described by Benjamin Bloom and his colleagues. Instruction that is mastery based places emphasis on a two- or three-phase cycle (such as pretest/ teach/test for mastery) that focuses instruction on teaching for mastery of selected learning outcomes. By way of contrast, a full-fledged corrective mastery learning approach places additional systematic emphasis on correction of errors through reteaching and retesting (such as pretest/teach/test/reteach to correct errors/retest/ teach/posttest) (Jones, Friedman, Tinzmann, and Cox 1985; Jones 1982). We have seen both general mastery-based and corrective mastery learning approaches that have worked successfully at inner-city schools when adequate and appropriate attention has been given to identification and correction of students' most important skill deficits and learning problems. Jones and Spady (1985) have discussed considerations involving implementation of mastery learning instruction within the context of curriculum alignment and outcomes-based education in large school districts.

2. *Successful inner-city schools utilize unusually effective arrangements for low-achieving students.* A central characteristic of successful inner-city schools is their willingness to adopt or devise unusually effective organizational arrangements for teaching low-achieving students, who initially constitute a majority or near majority of their enrollment. Teachers at inner-city schools have struggled for decades with the problems inherent in teaching classes with a high proportion of low achievers. For some teachers, the "solution" has been to pace instruction for the slowest student, making sure that nearly every student "keeps up" with the class, but meanwhile causing the class as a whole to fall further and further behind. For others, the response has been to pace instruction in accordance with the performance of the faster students, in effect leaving the lowest achievers to fend for themselves. Since neither response works well for most students, educators have alternately sought to introduce either continuous-progress approaches, in which each student proceeds individually or in small groups at his or her own rate, or homogeneous grouping approaches (within or across grade levels) that might allow for more efficient pacing.

Individualized and small group approaches can be very effective, but successful implementation requires enormous resources for planning, personnel, staff development, and materials (Scriven 1976). Consequently, these approaches have failed much more often than they have succeeded. Homogeneous grouping is an attractive alternative for many teachers and administrators, but, here too, implementation generally has been relatively unsuccessful. We will discuss these approaches further in the concluding part of this chapter, but at this point we want to emphasize several key considerations regarding the problems of homogeneous and heterogenous grouping.

(a) Some effective inner-city schools build instruction on homogeneous grouping, particularly in reading. Examples include some of the elementary schools in Community District 19 in Brooklyn, New York, which assign the lowest-achieving students to small "parallel" classes taught by outstanding teachers (Levine and Stark 1982), and certain schools elsewhere that use whole-class, mastery-learning reading instruction for students grouped within or across grade levels (Robb 1985).

(b) Grouping practices raise issues that are *par excellence* involved in determining whether mastery learning or other outcomes-based approaches are feasible and manageable for teachers. If there are more than three or four subgroups in a class, or if there is substantial spread within the subgroups, most teachers will not be able to deliver instruction effectively, unless they have much more resources, training, and assistance than most do now.

(c) Research suggests that the key variable in determining whether grouping will be effective is the total number of low-achieving students in the classroom. For example, recent research by Barr and Dreeben (1983) shows that teachers' decisions about organizing and delivering instruction depend not on the size of the class *per se* but on the size of the "low aptitude contingent of children" (p. 159). This conclusion is neither mysterious nor surprising. Teachers with many low-achieving students have a very difficult task, compared with other teachers, in assigning and monitoring constructive seatwork, in providing adequate time for skill mastery and corrective instruction, and in motivating students.

(d) One implication of the preceding discussion is that homogeneous grouping is more likely to work if low-achieving classes or groups are much smaller than other classes or groups and are taught by the most skilled teachers. Recent research also is clarifying other variables that are critical for successful homogeneous grouping. For example, Leinhardt and Pallay (1982) studied the literature on "restrictive settings" (that is, placement in separate groups for special education and compensatory education), and found that effective instruction in these settings depends, among other things, on efficient use of student and teacher time, a formal management system encouraging high task orientation, and positive teacher affect. Gamoran (1984) studied homogeneous grouping for reading within classrooms and found that results depended on whether teachers used "egalitarian" or "elitist" practices that either minimized or emphasized group distinctions. Neutral "naming" of groups, minimization of ability differences between groups, and provisions for cross-group contact were associated with high reading gains among students in initially low-achieving groups.

Workable decisions about arrangements for low achievers usually reflect an explicit distinction between students who are virtually nonreaders and those who can recognize and sound out words but cannot read with comprehension. This distinction becomes critically important in the third and fourth grades when instruction begins to emphasize independent understanding of text materials and when the presence of students who cannot read at all leads teachers to slow the pace of learning for the entire class. By the fifth or sixth grade, one also must also distinguish between and accommodate the needs of students who can decode words but read poorly and students reading at or above grade level. In the absence of these distinctions, traditional organizational arrangements will result in ineffective instruction that may be responsive to the situation of one or another subgroup (that is, nonreaders, low readers, average and good readers) but not the others.

3. *Successful inner-city schools provide coordinated instruction within and across classrooms and grade levels.* This generalization is particularly salient regarding reading, mathematics, and other basic skills. The importance of coordination arises from imperatives to provide sufficient time for students to master the most important skills, to ensure that instruction avoids common pitfalls and dangers (see below), and to provide consistency throughout the overall learning environment of inner-city students. Adequate coordination is provided by attending to at least three major aspects of instruction: (a) reduction or elimination of confusion and inconsistency in compensatory education arrangements; (b) coordination across grade levels; and (c) coordination of subject matter within the regular classroom.

(a) Reduction or elimination of confusion and inconsistency in compensatory education most often takes the form of revision or rejection of the most commonly used Chapter 1 approach—the "pullout" model. Rather than pulling low achievers out of class for supplementary instruction and thereby magnifying possibilities of inconsistent and contradictory methods and materials between regular and Chapter 1 instruction, many effective inner-city schools have placed the lowest achieving students in very small self-contained classes or in somewhat larger classes taught by two full-time teachers.

However, some inner-city schools have succeeded in providing adequate coordination of instruction within the pullout model. Though this is exceedingly difficult, these schools systematically coordinate instruction between regular and supplementary class-rooms. Several examples are described in a study by Levine and Stark (1981) and in a New York State study that contrasted a successful ("overachieving") inner-city school with an unsuccessful school and found that:

> Teachers in School A (overachieving) were required to remain with their classes in the Title I lab for in-service education purposes. The result was that the teachers interviewed could describe the activities planned for students in the reading laboratory. . . . On the other hand, teachers inter-viewed in the other school wondered what the students were doing in the reading laboratory. (State of New York 1974)

(b) The imperative of coordination across grade levels is asso-ciated with the need to provide outcomes-based instruction in the context of curriculum alignment and mastery learning. If instruction in basic skills is not well coordinated across grade levels, teachers tend to repeat skills many or most of their students already have mastered (because a few have not), to blame teachers in lower grades—as well as the students themselves—for students' skill deficiencies, or to emphasize "grade-level" skills for which students do not have prere-quisite entry knowledge. The overall result is to reinforce the prevail-ing and debilitating pattern wherein teachers "advance" students page by page through the textbook, with students falling further and further behind and teachers "absolving" themselves of responsibility by arguing that they "taught" the required textbook.

(c) Coordination of subject matter within the classroom is partic-ularly important in reading, where several hours of instruction each day typically are devoted to specific reading skills, writing, oral language, analysis of stories, and other language arts activities. In addition, instruction in social studies, science, and other subjects obviously can help develop and reinforce important reading skills.

Lack of coordination of instruction within the classroom is exacer-bated by the practices typically used by teachers who have too many low achievers to allow for effective teaching. In essence, many or most teachers in this situation rely on the use of workbooks and worksheets to keep students occupied while the teachers struggle with the learning problems of individuals or small groups. Regarding the quality and utility of workbooks in actually improving classroom instruction, Osborn, Jones, and Stein (1984) recently reported that workbook tasks are "troublesome" in the following respects:

> . . . the workbook tasks in some programs had little or nothing to do with what was going on in the rest of the program; the directions were often unclear, obscure, or unnecessarily lengthy; many of the tasks were trivial and had little or nothing to do with reading or writing. . . . some of the most important tasks were presented only once or twice. . . . [the vocabulary was complex] . . . the art and page layouts were confusing. (Pp. 42–43)

It should be noted that one of the central reasons for coordinating instruction is to attain a more rapid pacing of instruction. Since many inner-city students begin the school year two or three or more years below grade level, instruction obviously must be accelerated if they are to reduce this achievement gap. Thus effective schools projects must emphasize "accelerated pacing for full content coverage," as is done in the Milwaukee RISE project (McCormack-Larkin 1985).

4. *Instruction at inner-city schools must avoid dangers and pitfalls commonly encountered in implementing outcomes-based education.* There are hundreds, perhaps thousands, of pitfalls that can detrack efforts to implement outcomes-based instruction in the inner city. Many of these pitfalls involve technical issues in designing and implementing mastery learning. For example, Anderson and Jones (1981) have itemized a few of the major pitfalls in a mastery learning program as involving the following "failures" characteristic of "less-than-successful" programs: "Failure to . . . establish priorities among instructional objectives; . . . to organize objectives into instructional units and to order/sequence the units based on rational considerations . . . to properly orient students . . . [and] to make rational, justifiable decisions about performance standards" (pp. 122–123).

In our view, probably the most common and destructive general pitfall is the neglect or the de-emphasizing of the teaching of higher-order skills, particularly in homogeneous, low-achieving classes. Partly because some inner-city students need a great deal of help with lower-order skills, partly because these skills are much easier to teach and test, partly because teachers and administrators can make themselves look superficially effective by completing records showing student mastery of a multitude of low-level learning objectives, and for a host of other reasons, inner-city teachers typically place little practical emphasis on development of higher-order comprehension and thinking skills (Levine 1985). Our own case studies of successful inner-city elementary and intermediate schools indicate that, in one way or another, they concentrate on development of higher-order skills that help students learn to function more independently in the classroom and throughout the school (Eubanks and Levine 1983b, 1984; Levine, Levine, and Eubanks 1984). A related analysis is apparent in the successful RISE project in Milwaukee, where instructional improvement efforts systematically address the goals of "full content coverage" and "accelerated pacing" of learning. Arrangements for attaining these goals help educators at inner-city schools in the RISE project avoid getting bogged down on narrow, lower-order skills (McCormack-Larkin 1985).

A related danger that frequently subverts the effectiveness of instruction in inner-city schools is the common practice of "driving" instruction in unproductive directions suggested by tests that emphasize lower-level learning skills. To solve this problem, many districts and schools have attempted to base instruction on tests that diagnose students' learning problems and progress so that instruction can be redesigned to ensure more acceptable learning. Unfortunately, most tests have not been useful in directing instruction toward higher-order comprehension and thinking skills.

One major exception is the Degrees of Reading Power (DRP) Test recently developed by the College Board for use in grades four through twelve. The DRP is specifically designed to assess students' levels of comprehension of whole passages rather than individual words, phrases, or sentences (Cooper 1982). Since performance assessment units are related through a readability formula to the difficulty level of texts and other reading materials, one can identify materials appropriate for instruction that is designed to improve comprehension or, alternately, is suitable (that is nonfrustrating) for independent reading. We have seen several well-functioning inner-city schools in which instruction (beginning in the middle grades) is organized, first, around DRP assessment of students' and materials comprehension levels, and then on incorporation of teaching strategies selected to improve comprehensive skills. Thus, the DRP can facilitate a productive alignment of instructional objectives, materials, and teaching strategies, particularly at the secondary-school level where the emphasis of instruction should be on comprehension and higher-order thinking skills.

5. *Faculty at effective inner-city schools not only express allegiance to but "operationalize" shared values and goals, through instructional and organizational arrangements that improve students' learning.* By "operationalize" we mean that administrators and teachers do not simply express agreement that their students' achievement can and must be greatly improved, but move beyond this rhetoric to modify institutional arrangements even though doing so is certain to be personally difficult. In the absence of inconvenient and often painful change in instructional and organizational arrangements, agreement on the necessity for elements of effective education for disadvantaged students is merely "shared rhetoric" or, synonymously, "rhetorical consensus."

What kinds of arrangements and changes are operationalized at effective inner-city schools? It would be easy to list hundreds of institutional considerations that require attention and modification in efforts to improve achievement. Lacking space for such a list, we will limit our discussion to a summary of key "phenomena" or "factors" that Deborah Montgomery and Kenneth Leithwood (1983) of the Ontario Institute for Studies in Education have identified as being of particular "concern" to principals of unusually effective schools:

1. The determination of which teacher teaches which students.
2. The priorities and emphases among the objectives pursued by teachers as a focus for instruction.
3. The instructional strategies employed by teachers.
4. The instructional materials and resources used by teachers.
5. The nature and degree of integration among programs relative to the goals being pursued with students.

A somewhat similar analysis is provided by Coleman (1983).

Clearly, these concerns of effective principals focus substantially on the kinds of instructional considerations discussed in the preceding pages. What is not so obvious is that each of them requires difficult, sometimes ongoing adjustments by teachers and other faculty. Sarason (1978) shows how principals can provide collaborative leadership in developing and utilizing staff talents for this purpose. Instructional effectiveness frequently requires, among other things, that some teachers have larger classes than others, that experienced teachers work with the most difficult students, that teachers make less use of instructional materials they may have stockpiled and used comfortably for ten or twenty years, that extra time—often after school or during planning periods—be provided for teaching low achievers, that habitual practices in emphasizing or de-emphasizing social studies, science, or other subjects be greatly modified, that teachers assist each other in sequencing instruction across grades, and that instruction be accelerated beyond teachers' initial level of comfort. Initiation of effective arrangements and practices involving these and other related goals frequently requires circumvention or disregard of school board or teachers' union agreements, standing up to pressure and criticism from factions in the school, district, or community, and unpopular insistence that improved achievement is more important than personal preferences or vested interests of subgroups of teachers, parents, and administrators.

We should note that schools vary a great deal in the extent to which time and other resources must be expended in developing agreements to operationalize shared values that emphasize improved student achievement. At one extreme are a few schools in which there is true agreement that improved academic achievement takes precedence over existing institutional arrangements; here the problems of change management are largely technical. At the other extreme are schools in which lip service is given to the need for improvement, but faculty are unwilling to modify most existing practices; here initial intervention should concentrate on development of a consensus strong enough to allow for systematic change in organizational and instructional arrangements. In this case successful improvement efforts may require a large-scale organizational development (OD) effort utilizing a cadre of specialists who work with faculty in "such areas as communication skills, problem-solving, conflict resolution, decision-making, and goal identification. . . .[and help them examine their] customary ways of working together in meetings, or the ways in which people are linked together to get their daily work done" (ERIC Clearinghouse on Educational Management 1984).

We also should emphasize that shared goals and values are most likely to be developed and operationalized when faculty possess and analyze concrete data that underline the need for coordinated changes in instructional and organizational arrangements. Usable data of this sort go beyond information showing that students in a given school have very low achievement—a fact that everyone already knows and that frequently serves more to generate frustration and recrimination than to encourage constructive change. Data collected to improve school functioning should extend to the classroom level, should bear in one way or another on instructional practice, and should implicitly point the way toward possible improvements in instructional arrangements. Among the (at least occasionally) successful approaches for collecting such data that we have seen used in school effectiveness projects are the following:

(a) DRP data (as explained above) that force teachers to confront the conclusion that they are using inappropriate instructional materials.

(b) Teacher Expectations and Student Achievement (TESA) data that are collected by teachers through peer observation and highlight undesirable and unproductive instructional orientations toward low achievers.

(c) Self-assessment and peer assessment data collected through Jane Stallings's classroom snapshot techniques.

(d) Instruments such as the one used by the Mid-Continent Regional Educational Laboratory to measure Academic Learning Time.

(e) "Comparative monitoring of classroom progress" charts that teachers use to assess students' progress through an aligned curriculum in differing classes with approximately the same initial performance level at a given grade level (Levine and Eubanks 1983).

6. *Instructional improvement activities at effective inner-city schools are implemented organically rather than bureaucratically.* We use the term "organic

implementation" as a contrast to bureaucratic approaches that attempt to improve instruction through directives and detailed, written specifications. Instructional innovations are bureaucratic when they are mandated in detail, every step in delivering instruction is specified and must be followed precisely, and compliance is monitored largely through elaborate check-off mechanisms with highly prescribed enumeration of activities. Recent thinking in organizational theory stresses that formal organizations seldom succeed in accomplishing their goals through the traditional bureaucratic approach; instead, analysts believe that success in innovation requires adaptation of technical approaches to unique circumstances, tolerance of deviation from a master plan, assessment and monitoring of progress through personal observation rather than ritual tabulation of data reflecting superficial compliance with directives, and possibilities for coupling units or subunits through interpersonal cooperation rather than memos and check sheets (Weick 1979).

By way of contrast, implementation of instructional improvement is organic when teachers and administrators not only depart from but are encouraged and assisted to depart from general guidelines in order to achieve the overall purposes of the instructional program, and when administrative directives are reduced to a minimum in favor of collegial teacher planning and decision making with close and personal support from administrators and supervisors. A good example of the importance of organic as opposed to bureaucratic or mechanical implementation has been provided by a study that Shirley Jackson (1982) conducted in the Washington, D.C., public schools. Jackson compared several elementary schools that were effective for "low socioeconomic urban black students" with others that were not effective, and found that the former group were more flexible in adapting the district's Comprehensive Basic Curriculum (CBC). The effective schools, she reported, place

> . . . a great deal of emphasis on raising test scores and they will go outside of the CBC when necessary, that is, they are not totally limited or controlled by the CBC materials suggested in the guide. Subjects in ineffective schools are also dedicated to meeting the CBC objectives but seem to be controlled by the mechanics and management aspects of the system rather than letting the instructional needs of the students be the driving force. (P. 171)

7. *Components of the overall instructional approach must be carefully selected to form a unified whole, particularly with reference to whether the general goal is to be incremental improvement or fundamental reform of instruction.* Throughout this chapter we have cited and illustrated a variety of successful practices and approaches that have improved instruction at inner-city schools. There are many ways to bring about improved instruction, provided that one attends to the topics and considerations discussed in the preceding pages. A summary of these themes is provided in Figure 4–1.

Examination of Figure 4–1 makes it apparent that the instructional dimensions and considerations we have discussed are highly interrelated. For example, outcomes-based instruction involves effective curriculum alignment and some form of mastery learning, but successful implementation of an aligned curriculum also depends on effective arrangements for grouping students, coordination of instruction across and within grades and classrooms, and avoidance of pitfalls in mastery learning. Similarly, it is apparent that one cannot coordinate instruction very well unless faculty operationalize agreements regarding their teaching responsibilities. Appropriate data must be collected in order to assess the delivery of an aligned curriculum, the workability of arrangements for low achievers, and the problems encountered in mastery learning.

One could easily rearrange the headings and themes discussed in this chapter (and in Figure 4–1) by using some alternate framework for classification. For example, aspects of instructional coordination could be discussed primarily under the theme *outcomes-based instruction*, and grouping of students could be discussed primarily with regard to *operationalization of shared values*. We invite readers either to reorganize or add to our headings, thereby possibly devising a more useful way of identifying and discussing dimensions of instructional effectiveness at inner-city schools. We also invite you to add examples of successful activities and approaches, and we welcome your suggestions regarding other modification or expansion of Figure 4–1. We obviously are not arguing that the activities and approaches cited in the text and Figure 4–1 constitute the only means for raising achievement, but we do believe that each of the dimensions listed in the figure must be

Figure 4–1
Examples of Activities and Approaches Emphasized at Successful Inner-City Schools*

Effectiveness Dimension	*Major Considerations and Illustrative Activities and Approaches*
I. *Outcomes-based instruction*	1. *Curriculum alignment* —Los Angeles Curriculum Alignment Project —Chicago Mastery Learning Reading 2. *Mastery learning* —Mastery-based —Corrective mastery
II. *Effective arrangements for low achievers*	1. *Grouping* —Homogeneous with whole-class emphasis —Heterogeneous with individual or small-group emphasis 2. *Distinction between nonreaders, poor readers, and competent readers*
III. *Coordination of instruction*	1. *Consistency with compensatory education* 2. *Coordination across grade levels* 3. *Coordination of subject matter within classrooms*
IV. *Avoidance of pitfalls*	1. *Technical issues in mastery learning* 2. *Emphasis on higher-order skills***
V. *Operationalization of shared values*	1. *Distribution of students and resources, time for learning, and so on* 2. *Organizational development* 3. *Collection of appropriate data* —Degrees of reading power (DRP) —TESA —Stallings's snapshots —Academic Learning Time analysis —Comparative monitoring of classroom progress
VI. *Organic implementation*	1. *Personal support for teachers rather than bureaucratic usage of check-sheets* 2. *Flexibility in adapting mandates*

* Dimensions, considerations, and activities and approaches emphasized at successful inner-city schools are discussed in the text.

** Approaches that we have seen used successfully to emphasize higher-order skills include: (1) utilization of the Degrees of Reading Power (DRP) test to align curriculum and instruction; (2) systematic use of Bloom's taxonomy in designing instruction; and (3) use of the Chicago Mastery Learning Reading Program or other similar materials emphasizing comprehension skills.

---

attended to in some meaningful and systematic fashion if achievement is to be substantially improved.

We also want to call attention explicitly to part II, no. 1 in Figure 4–1, which indicates that either heterogeneous or homogeneous grouping can provide the basis for instructional improvement at inner-city schools. Either approach can be implemented successfully, but as mentioned above, heterogeneous grouping generally emphasizes individual and small-group instruction and requires very large resources, while homogeneous grouping (when successful) allows for a greater emphasis on teacher-centered, whole-class instruction. Stress on whole-class instruction reduces opportunities to provide the kind of individual attention required to help inner-city students make very large gains in a very short period of time. On the other hand, an individual or small-group approach requires much more change throughout the school (involving schedules, sequencing of materials, frequent reassignment of students and teachers, and the like) than does homogeneous grouping emphasizing whole-class instruction. For these reasons, we view approaches that emphasize heterogeneous grouping and individual or small-group instruction as involving *fundamental reform* of a school, while emphasis on homogeneous grouping and whole-class instruction tends to allow for *incremental improvement*. The latter is relatively easy to initiate but yields smaller gains in achievement than a successful fundamental reform approach.

Similarly, we believe that a *holistic* emphasis in instruction also constitutes a fundamental reform strategy, whereas an emphasis on mastery of specific skills generally is an incremental improvement approach. As described by Dorothy Strickland (1983) and others, a holistic approach in reading is one that stresses the goal of *meaning* rather than *decoding*, through direct acquisition of meaning from print without recoding into spoken language. By way of contrast, a "skills" approach (Strickland uses the term "subskills") stresses mastery of specific skills until the student can process print automatically. As Strickland points out, many theorists reject both "extreme" positions in favor of an interactive approach that "allows for more eclectic instructional procedures, using valuable insights and activities from both the holistic and subskills models" (p. 119).

Nevertheless, in practice effective inner-city schools tend to place greater or lesser emphasis on either the holistic or the subskills approach, and some go quite far in one direction or the other. Many of those that stress the holistic approach concentrate on integrating instruction across language arts, social studies, art, and other subjects in order to provide and encourage reading for the acquisition of meaning (see Comer [1980] for a good example), while those that stress the skills approach generally are exemplary mastery learning sites. In both cases attention must be paid to distinguishing between and providing appropriate learning experiences for both nonreaders and readers and, as indicated above, to higher-order comprehension skills. But because the holistic approach requires larger changes in what most teachers do and also requires students to read on their own much of the time (thus leading to stress on individual and small-group learning), it usually requires *fundamental reform* of instruction throughout the school (Goodman and Goodman 1982).

We have tried to summarize our view of these approaches in Figure 4–2, which portrays some differences between incremental improvement and fundamental reform of instruction. As shown in the figure, a fundamental reform school is one in which substantial changes and improvements in instructional arrangements (such as continuous progress; individualization) or holistic instruction have been effectively implemented throughout the school, resulting in large student achievement gains. In our experience, fundamental reform—in the few cases where it has been accomplished—typically requires years of organizational development and renewal, during which time administrators and teachers systematically examine and revise all aspects of organization functioning. By way of contrast, incremental improvement tends to be the pattern in multischool projects that attempt to bring about significant improvement in a group of inner-city schools. Good examples of incremental, multi-school reform are the RISE project, which includes eighteen elementary schools in Milwaukee, and New York City's School Improvement Project. A preliminary look at these projects indicates that although (more correctly, *because*) they do not initially attempt to thoroughly reform all aspects of a school's organization and functioning, they represent a relatively manageable approach to multischool reform and result in significant achievement gains in most participating schools within one or two years (Eubanks and Levine 1983a).

Attempts to introduce fundamental reform at a fairly large number of schools within one or two years generally have been disastrous. In addition to requiring very large amounts of time and other resources, fundamental reform probably requires a specially selected administrator and some degree of selection of teachers and other staff, particularly in order to "shake out" personnel who are not willing or able to participate in the very difficult process of defining and implementing radically different instructional arrangements such as continuous progress or individualization. For example, to ask or expect teachers in the average school to totally revise instructional arrangements with limited resources in a relatively short time period constitutes an invitation to chaos. Two decades of attempted innovation in education have shown that fundamental reform is not a task to be undertaken with limited material and human resources.

To those readers who respond that inner-city schools *must* provide holistic instruction emphasizing comprehension and other higher-order skills across subject areas if their students are to reach or exceed national achievement averages above the third or fourth grades, we can only say that we agree. The important underlying issue, in our view, is how one gets from here to there. It is possible to reach this goal either by fundamentally reforming all aspects of instruction (as some inner-city schools have done) or by initiating more limited (that is, incremental) improvements in learning and climate and then moving beyond this level to more fundamental reform. Whether either approach will succeed depends, to some extent, on ongoing analysis that particularly ensures that adequate resources are in place to allow for successful implementation of whichever approach one chooses to take in working to improve achievement at inner-city schools.

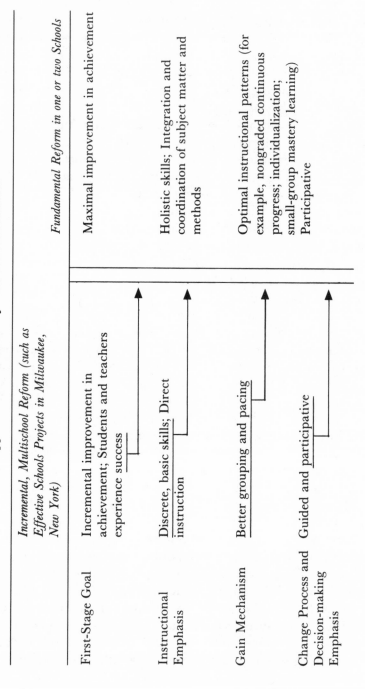

Figure 4–2
Two Approaches to Inner-City Instructional Reform*

	Incremental, Multischool Reform (such as Effective Schools Projects in Milwaukee, New York)	Fundamental Reform in one or two Schools
First-Stage Goal	Incremental improvement in achievement; Students and teachers experience success	Maximal improvement in achievement
Instructional Emphasis	Discrete, basic skills; Direct instruction	Holistic skills; Integration and coordination of subject matter and methods
Gain Mechanism	Better grouping and pacing	Optimal instructional patterns (for example, nongraded continuous progress; individualization; small-group mastery learning)
Change Process and Decision-making Emphasis	Guided and participative	Participative

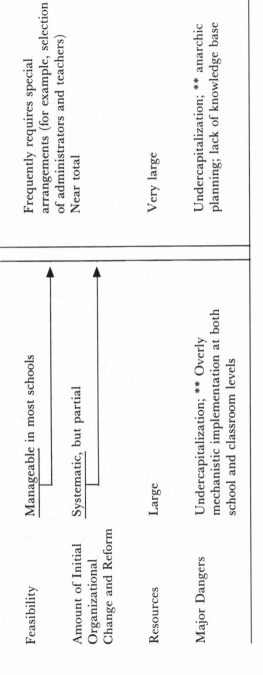

Feasibility	Manageable in most schools	Frequently requires special arrangements (for example, selection of administrators and teachers)
Amount of Initial Organizational Change and Reform	Systematic, but partial	Near total
Resources	Large	Very large
Major Dangers	Undercapitalization; ** Overly mechanistic implementation at both school and classroom levels	Undercapitalization; ** anarchic planning; lack of knowledge base

* Possible steps (see text) to move to incremental reform and beyond: productive direct instruction, curriculum alignment, site-level training, reduce or eliminate pull-out, outcome-based supervision. Double line refers to "take-off" stage at which schools might move from incremental improvement to fundamental reform. Underlined characteristics indicate incremental changes that enhance schools' capacity to reform and innovate successfully.

** Capitalization refers to both material and human resources.

CONCLUDING REMARKS

Because space limitations prevent us from discussing many other topics that are important in efforts to improve instruction at inner-city schools, we want to at least briefly mention several that are particularly critical in determining whether such efforts succeed or fail.

1. It is well known that administrative leadership, particularly on the part of the building principal, frequently is the crucial characteristic associated with successful inner-city schools. Leadership of the principal has been considered a key variable in research and analysis beginning in the 1960s (Doll 1969) and extending through important studies published during the past few years (Sizemore, Brossard, and Harrigan 1983; Morris, Crowson, Hurwitz, and Porter-Gehrie 1981). What has not been very clear is what the principal and other administrators do *vis-á-vis* instruction to improve achievement substantially. Stated differently, a few "maverick" principals successfully improved achievement in the inner city, but relatively little was known about what others should do regarding instruction to replicate their success.

As mentioned earlier, recent research has identified some of the instructional issues that effective principals are most concerned with, regardless of what type of school they manage (Montgomery and Leithwood 1983). Even more pertinent for this chapter, we now know a fair amount about instructional and organizational arrangements and their implementation at successful inner-city schools. The instructional dimensions and considerations described in this chapter are among those that inner-city administrators must address systematically if they hope to make their schools substantially more effective.

2. Effective instruction at inner-city schools should take into account the learning styles of economically disadvantaged students. Although efforts to systematically differentiate instruction according to learning style differences generally have not resulted in substantial gains in achievement (Chiarelott and Davidman 1983), research and experience indicate that certain instructional approaches involving students' learning styles can help make inner-city schools effective. For example, considerable research supports the conclusion that Student Team Learning (STL) and other forms of cooperative learning are particularly suited to the learning style of many disadvantaged students and can help produce large achievement gains (Slavin 1983).

Similarly, relatively simple guidelines requiring teachers to provide corrective mastery instruction in a mode (for example, visual, aural) different from initial instruction appear to be of great value in implementing mastery learning for students initially low in achievement (Mamary and Rowe 1985), probably in part because this approach is at least partially responsive to learning style differences among disadvantaged students.

3. Efforts to improve the effectiveness of instruction at the secondary level generally require structural change in the school as a whole. Although we believe that the generalizations described in this chapter are as relevant at the secondary as the elementary level, intermediate schools and high schools are complex institutions that must be structurally modified if instructional improvements are to be implemented effectively. By "structural change" we mean extensive, schoolwide changes in practices regarding subjects taught, scheduling of classes, and allocation of students to teachers. Without major changes in schedules, grouping, and teacher responsibilities, secondary faculty generally will be unable to develop and implement effective outcomes-based programs for inner-city students (Levine and Sherk 1983; Levine, Levine, and Eubanks 1985).

4. Finally, we should emphasize the importance of several *implementation prerequisites* for improving instruction at inner-city schools. Having examined instructional improvement efforts in Chicago, Kansas City, Los Angeles, Milwaukee, New York, and other cities, we believe that these prerequisites include: (a) instructional-resource personnel who work with teachers in the classroom on a full-time basis (at least one full-time person for every fifteen to twenty teachers); (b) adequate staff development and collegial planning time scheduled regularly (at least once a week) as part of the regular school day; and (c) help from a sufficient number of supportive personnel such as teacher aides, parent volunteers, and future teachers to provide teachers with "assured availability" of appropriate instructional materials in reading, mathematics, and other subjects (Levine and Stark 1982). In the absence of these prerequisites, teachers seldom are able to cope with the massive, day-to-day challenges involved in substantially improving the achievement of students at inner-city schools.

REFERENCES

Anderson, Lorin, and Jones, Beau Fly. "Designing Instructional Strategies Which Facilitate Learning for Mastery." *Educational Psychologist* 16 (Autumn 1981): 122–123.

Barr, Rebecca, and Dreeben, Robert. *How Schools Work*. Chicago: University of Chicago Press, 1983.

Chiarelott, Leigh, and Davidman, Leonard. "Learning Style Inventories: Implications for Curriculum and Instruction." Paper presented at the Annual Meeting of the American Educational Research Association, Montreal, 1983.

Coleman, Peter. "Towards More Effective Schools: Improving Elementary Schools." *Administrator's Notebook* 21, no. 4 (1983): 1–4.

Comer, James. *School Power*. New York: Free Press, 1980.

Cooper, Eric J. "DRP Adopted in Boston." *College Board News*, Fall 1982.

Doll, Russell C. *Variations among Inner-City Elementary Schools*. Kansas City: University of Missouri, 1969.

ERIC Clearinghouse on Educational Management. "The Culture of an Effective School." Research Action Brief No. 22. Eugene, Oregon: ERIC Clearinghouse on Educational Management, 1984.

Eubanks, Eugene E., and Levine, Daniel U. "A First Look at Effective School Projects at Inner-City Elementary Schools." Paper presented at the Annual Meeting of the American Association of School Administrators, Atlantic City, 1983 (a).

Eubanks, Eugene E., and Levine, Daniel U. "A First Look at Effective School Projects in New York City and Milwaukee." *Phi Delta Kappan* 64 (June 1983): 697–702 (b).

Eubanks, Eugene E., and Levine, Daniel U. "Effective Inner-City Elementary Schools." *Social Policy* 15 (Fall 1984): 4–29.

Gamoran, Adam. "Egalitarian Versus Elitist Use of Ability Grouping." Paper presented at the Annual Meeting of the American Educational Research Association, New Orleans, 1984.

Goodman, Kenneth S., and Goodman, Yetta M. "A Whole Language Comprehension-Centered View of Reading Development." In *Basic Skills Issues and Choices*, vol. 2, edited by Linda Reed and Spencer Ward. St. Louis: CEMREL, 1982.

Jackson, Shirley Crite. "Instructional Leadership Behaviors that Characterize Schools that Are Effective for Low Socioeconomic Black Students." Ph.D. dissertation, Catholic University of America, 1982.

Jones, Beau Fly, "Key Management Decisions for Implementing Mastery Learning." *School Administrator* 39 (March 1982): 45–48.

Jones, Beau Fly; Friedman, Lawrence B.; Tinzmann, Margaret; and Cox, Beverly E. "Guidelines for Instruction-Enriched Mastery Learning to Improve Comprehension." In *Improving Student Achievement through Mastery Learning Programs*, edited by Daniel U. Levine. San Francisco: Jossey-Bass, 1985.

Jones, Beau Fly, and Spady, William G. "Enhanced Mastery Learning and Quality of Instruction." In *Improving Student Achievement through Mastery Learning Programs*, edited by Daniel U. Levine. San Francisco: Jossey-Bass, 1985.

Leinhardt, Gaea, and Pallay, Allan. "Restrictive Educational Settings: Exile or Haven?" *Review of Educational Research* 52 (Winter 1982): 557–578.

Levine, Daniel U., ed. *Improving Student Achievement through Mastery Learning Programs*. San Francisco: Jossey-Bass, 1985.

Levine, Daniel U., and Eubanks, Eugene E. "Instructional and Organizational Arrangements at an Unusually Effective Inner-City Elementary School in Chicago." Paper presented at the Annual Meeting of the American Educational Research Association, Montreal, 1983.

Levine, Daniel U.; Levine, Reyna F.; and Eubanks, Eugene F. "Characteristics of Effective Inner-City Intermediate Schools." *Phi Delta Kappan* 65 (June 1984): 707–711.

Levine, Daniel U.; Levine, Rayna F.; and Ornstein, Allan O. "Guidelines for Change and Innovation in the Secondary School Curriculum." *NASSP Bulletin* 69 (May 1985): 9–14.

Levine, Daniel U., and Sherk, John S. "Organizational Arrangements to Increase Productive Time for Reading in High Schools." Paper prepared for the International Reading Association, November 1983.

Levine, Daniel U., and Stark, Joyce. *Instructional and Organizational Arrangements and Processes for Improving Academic Achievement at Inner-City Elementary Schools*. Kansas City: University of Missouri, 1981. NIE-G-81-0070.

Levine, Daniel U., and Stark, Joyce. "Instructional and Organizational Arrangements that Improve Achievement in Inner-City Schools." *Educational Leadership* 40 (December 1982): 41–46.

Mamary, Albert, and Rowe, Larry A. "Flexible and Heterogeneous Arrangements to Facilitate Mastery Learning." In *Improving Student Achievement through Mastery Learning Programs*, edited by Daniel U. Levine. San Francisco: Jossey-Bass, 1985.

McCormack-Larkin, Maureen. "Ingredients of a Successful School Effectiveness Project." *Educational Leadership* 42 (March 1985): 31–37.

Montgomery, Deborah J., and Leithwood, Kenneth A. "Evaluating Curriculum Implementation: A Critical Task for the Effective Principal." Paper presented at the Annual Meeting of the American Educational Research Association, Montreal, 1983.

Morris, Van Cleve; Crowson, Robert L.; Hurwitz, Emanuel, Jr.; and Porter-Gehrie, Cynthia. *The Urban Principal*. Chicago: University of Illinois at Chicago, 1981.

Niedermeyer, Fred, and Yelon, Steven. "Los Angeles Aligns Instruction with Essential Skills." *Educational Leadership* 38 (May 1981): 618–620.

Osborn, Jean; Jones, Beau Fly; and Stein, Mary. "The Case for Improving Textbook Programs: An Issue of Quality." In *Excellence in Our Schools: Making It Happen*. San Francisco: College Board and Far West Laboratory, 1984.

Robb, Donald W. "Strategies for Implementing Successful Mastery Learning Programs: Case Studies." In *Improving Student Achievement through Mastery Learning*

Programs, edited by Daniel U. Levine. San Francisco: Jossey-Bass, 1985.

Sarason, Seymour B. *The Creation of Settings and Future Societies.* San Francisco: Jossey-Bass, 1978.

Scriven, Michael. "Problems and Prospects for Individualization." In *Systems of Individualized Education*, edited by Harriet Talmage. Berkeley, Calif.: McCutchan Publishing Corp., 1976.

Sizemore, Barbara A.; Brossard, Carlos A.; and Harrigan, Birney. *An Abashing Anomaly: The High Achieving Predominantly Black Elementary School.* Pittsburgh: University of Pittsburgh, 1983.

Slavin, Robert. *Cooperative Learning.* New York: Longman, 1983.

State of New York. *School Factors Influencing Reading Achievement: A Case Study of Two Inner-City Schools.* Albany, N.Y.: Office of Performance Review, New York State Department of Education, 1974.

Strickland, Dorothy S. "The Development of Language and Literacy: Essential Knowledge for Teaching and Learning." In *Essential Knowledge for Beginning Educators*, edited by David C. Smith. Washington, D.C.: ERIC Clearinghouse on Teacher Education, 1983.

Weick, Karl. *The Social Psychology of Organizing.* Reading, Mass.: Addison-Wesley, 1979.

5

Effective High Schools: What Are Their Attributes?

Samuel Peng

Educational researchers and policymakers as well as the general public want to know what kinds of schools are most effective in fostering excellence in education. What makes one school better than another? Is it school facilities, teachers, curricular programs, school control, or student-body composition? Answers to these questions may help identify the best ways for improving education; may shed light on such matters as students' declining test scores, school crime, and discipline problems; and could provide a basis on which parents might choose one school over another for their children.

While many researchers have addressed these concerns, their answers have not always been consistent. In the late 1960s and early 1970s a number of researchers concluded that school variables have little impact on student learning after student home environment and mental ability are taken into account (see, for example, Coleman et al. 1966; Jencks et al. 1973; Jensen 1969; Averch et al. 1972). In recent years, however, several researchers have reported contrary findings to the effect that school variables, as well as student and home variables, do influence student outcomes (Bridge, Judd, and Moock 1979; Rutter, Maughan, Mortimore, and Ouston 1979; Brookover et al. 1979; Madaus, Airasian, and Kellaghan 1980). For example, Bridge and colleagues (1979), after a review of fifteen years of input-output research in education, concluded that "many characteristics of schools, teachers, and student bodies have been found consistently to affect educational outcomes. Admittedly, these inputs may have relatively smaller effects than do the characteristics of families and individuals, yet these inputs are subject to the control of policymakers and therefore deserve attention" (p. 286). Madaus and colleagues (1980) concluded that "a school climate characterized by social rewards for academic excellence, where discipline and scholastic achievement are valued by teachers and students, and teaching and learning are structured and focused on scholastic goals, contributes to high student achievement" (p. 189). Other studies indicate that the amount of homework required (Takai 1982) and the number of mathematics courses taken (Welch, Anderson, and Harris 1982) significantly account for differences among students' test scores.

The lack of consistent findings on the impact of school variables may result from the ever-changing process of teaching and learning and from the lack of comparability among certain studies. Nevertheless, it indicates the need for a systematic study to address the questions raised earlier—a study that takes into account differences in home background, in-school variations, and the initial ability of the students when they enter school and includes test scores and other student behaviors as outcome measures of schooling.

A recent national survey entitled "High School and Beyond" (HS&B) has provided an opportunity to carry out such a study. HS&B is a longitudinal survey sponsored by the National Center for Education Statistics, within the Office of Educational Research and Improvement, U.S. Department of Education. The survey used a national probability sample of 1,015 schools with up to 36 sophomores and 36 seniors randomly selected in each school. In spring 1980, an administrator in each sample school completed a questionnaire about characteristics and practices in his or her school. Students completed a questionnaire and a battery of tests in several subjects, including reading, vocabulary, mathematics, and science. The school and student surveys together yielded a comprehensive data base for examining the relationship between school characteristics and student outcome measures.

This chapter describes the study we designed to analyze the data from the "High School and Beyond" survey. The primary purpose of this study is to investigate the questions of whether schools make a difference in students' scores on achievement tests and other behavior measures and whether such school variables as curricular programs, discipline rules, school practices, teacher characteristics, and social, psychological, and physical environments significantly account for the differences.

CONCEPTUALIZATION OF THE PROCESS OF EDUCATION

To address these questions, it is helpful first to conceptualize how a school brings about student learning. The process is complex. It involves interrelated resources and events that are intended to motivate, shape, and elicit certain student behaviors and educational outcomes. This process is depicted in Figure 5–1. Clusters of related variables are boxed, and the arrows indicate the direction of the functional relationships.

The process, as shown in Figure 5–1, depicts the relationships within and among three types of variables: school variables, student-body attributes, and student behaviors. School variables include school policies, school resources, and school practices. They generally define what a school attempts to provide. Student-body attributes indicate what students bring into the school. To a large extent, they reflect students' home backgrounds and other socioeconomic characteristics. Both types of variables will independently and jointly affect the outcome of education as measured by student behaviors.

Probably most important in determining the character of a school is its policies regarding administrative procedures, educational goals, graduation requirements, standards of student conduct, and the like. To some extent, these policies reflect the values of the community and set directions for allocating school resources and for determining school practices. In this study, school policies are represented by some direct measures, such as the use of minimum competency requirements for graduation, and some proxy measures, such as type of control (public or private). These variables, however, may not accurately reflect all of the variations in policies among schools. For example, differences in school autonomy are probably greater among public schools than between public and private schools.

School study resources include school facilities, student-teacher

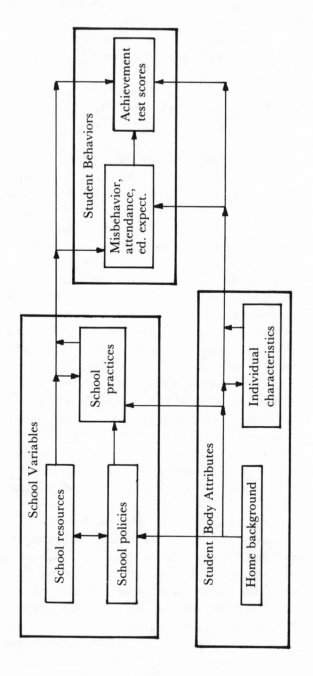

Figure 5-1
Process of School Education

ratio, teacher qualifications, school size, and the number and kinds of courses offered by the school. It is assumed that better resources provide greater opportunities for students to learn. Better resources may also help to create a psychological environment conducive to learning.

School practices refer to the ways that school policies are implemented in the effort to give students meaningful educational experiences. This study examines the following school practices: type of curriculum, school rules and their degree of enforcement, amount of homework, extracurricular activities, and specific instructional procedures such as ability grouping and remedial work for slower learners.

While these school variables will greatly influence the nature and the quality of a school, the type of students enrolled in the school is also a potent influence. Previous studies have shown that such student-body attributes as racial composition, family background, parental expectation, and parental involvement in school have a significant impact on student performance (Averch et al. 1972). These attributes not only are related to the individual's ability and aspirations but also can create a type of peer-group subculture that influences student behavior and learning.

Student behaviors are assumed to be partially the result of the particular instructions and guidance students have received. In most educational research the outcome is measured by scores on achievement tests. This study utilizes not only test scores but also measures of school attendance, educational expectations, and student misbehavior. These behavior measures are assumed to be related to test scores.

To summarize, education is a process that involves many interrelated variables. It is hypothesized that many of these variables can be used to characterize those schools where students exhibit desirable behavior patterns and achieve high test scores. The variables included in the study are listed in Table 5–1. Their definitions and measurement scales are presented in Appendix 5–1.

ANALYSIS STRATEGIES

We will next describe certain general features of the analysis strategy, which were necessary because of the complexity of the issues investigated.

Table 5–1
Variables Affecting Education

School Variables	
School policies:	school type (public or private), minimum competency requirements
School resources:	school size, quality of facilities, student-teacher ratio, percentage of teachers with advanced degrees, teacher turnover rate, number of courses offered
School practices:	curricular program, number of discipline rules, effectiveness and fairness of discipline, ability grouping, amount of homework, extracurricular activities, total hours in school-year
Student-Body Attributes	
Family background:	socioeconomic status, parental involvement, parental press
Student characteristics:	percentage of black or Hispanic students
Student Outcomes	
Test scores:	composite of reading, vocabulary, and mathematics test scores
Other behaviors:	school attendance, misbehavior, educational expectations

The Use of Schools Instead of Individual Students as the Unit of Analysis

Since the focus of the study is on identifying the characteristics of effective schools, schools rather than individual students were used as the unit of analysis. This presented no major problems. Most of the school data were obtained from school administrators or their designated representatives. The student data that were aggregated to represent a school provided unbiased estimates because students in each school were randomly selected. It should also be noted that the number of students in each school was sufficiently large to provide reliable estimates (up to 36 seniors and 36 sophomores per school).

The Use of Composite Rather than Individual Test Scores

In view of the fact that the HS&B tests are relatively short, the scores on three tests (reading, vocabulary, and mathematics) were combined to maximize their overall validity and reliability. The mean composite score within each school was used in the analysis.

The Use of Sophomore Data as Proxy Measures for Seniors' Entry Level

In examining the effects of school characteristics on the achievement of seniors, it is necessary to control for differences between schools in the initial achievement levels of their beginning students. Since initial achievement levels of seniors are unknown, the scores of the *sophomores* were used as proxies and as a covariate in the analyses.

RESULTS

Do Schools Make a Difference?

The means, standard deviations, and simple correlation coefficients between predictor and outcome variables are shown in Table 5–2. All student-body attributes are highly related to senior test scores; the simple correlation coefficients range from 0.35 for parental press to 0.76 for socioeconomic status. (Correlation coefficients can range from 1.00 in the case of a perfect positive linear association to −1.00 in the case of a perfect negative linear association between predictor and outcome variables.) However, many school variables such as school type, facilities, courses offered, curricular program, amount of homework, effectiveness of discipline, and extracurricular activities also are significantly related to test scores ($r > 0.20$). Similar relationships exist between the predictor variables and educational expectations. However, the relationships between the predictor variables and student absenteeism as well as misbehavior are generally weak but are in expected directions. For example, students in academic programs and in schools where discipline was considered effective are less likely than other students to report misbehavior and to be absent.

The above descriptive statistics give some indications of the predictive power of individual variables. A question of interest is, How important are school variables in determining student behavior

Table 5–2

Means and Standard Deviations (SD) of Variables and Simple Correlation Coefficient Between Predictor and Outcome Variables

Predictor Variable[1]	Sample Size[2]	Mean	SD	Correlation coefficient[3]			
				Exp.	Abs.	Misb.	Test
Student-Body Attributes							
Average SES	1,015	−.07	.42	.72	.17	−.13	.76
Parental involvement	983	2.58	.77	.34	−.06	−.13	.44
Parental press	992	15.51	1.11	.72	.09	.15	.35
% black or Hispanic	959	14.58	24.54	.07	.06	.18	−.46
School Variables							
School type (public=1)	1,015	.77	.42	−.50	.04	.05	−.37
Competency requirements	976	.18	.38	.09	.09	.05	.06
School size	927	632	642	.16	.21	−.05	.06
Facilities	988	3.81	2.02	.34	.06	−.06	.28
Student–teacher ratio	925	13.23	14.61	−.03	−.02	.05	−.02
% teachers M.A., M.S., Ph.D.	963	37.80	22.92	.29	−.03	−.03	.19
Teacher turnover rate	972	11.14	14.34	−.05	.05	.19	−.09
# mathematics, science courses	988	4.96	1.24	.32	−.10	−.13	.42
# other courses	988	7.21	2.80	.23	.14	−.09	.28
Total hours in school year	988	825.29	226.97	−.10	−.09	−.12	−.11
Curriculum (academic=1)	992	.35	.26	.77	−.10	−.22	.68
Discipline rules	988	2.43	.67	.00	−.17	.01	.01
Effective discipline	1,015	2.36	.28	.25	−.12	−.17	.20
Ability grouping	976	.82	.88	.11	.12	−.02	.05
Amount of homework	992	3.45	1.31	.56	−.15	−.13	.46
Activity–intellectual	992	1.26	.56	.17	−.14	−.03	.03
Activity–artistic	992	.77	.40	.16	−.20	−.18	.20
Activity–sport	992	1.18	.42	.28	−.13	.00	.30
Activity–community	992	1.25	.54	−.17	−.18	−.11	−.21
Student Behavior— Entry Measures							
Educational expectation	1,001	14.59	1.07	.76	−.03	−.08	.57
Absenteeism	1,001	50.14	3.70	−.06	.70	.27	−.19
Misbehavior	1,001	49.44	2.14	−.25	.26	.40	−.28
Sophomore test	973	50.09	4.36	.57	−.10	−.27	.84
Student Behavior— Outcomes Measures							
Educational expectation	992	14.77	1.11		.00	−.23	.68
Absenteeism	992	49.93	3.27	.00		.23	−.07
Misbehavior	992	49.85	2.04	−.23	.23		−.34
Senior test	963	49.50	4.42	.68	−.07	−.34	

[1] Variables are defined in Appendix 5–1.

[2] The number of schools that had data for some of the selected variables is less than 1,015 due to item nonresponse or because some schools in the sample did not have senior classes in 1980 (992 had senior class).

[3] $r > 0.07$ or < -0.07 is significant at the 0.05 level.

Exp. = educational expectation
Abs. = absenteeism
Misb. = Misbehavior
Test = Senior test scores

after student-body attributes are accounted for? To answer this question, multiple regression analysis was performed by first entering student-body attributes and then determining the contribution of school variables and other student variables. The results are presented in Table 5–3.. Student-body attributes and sophomore test scores (as proxy measures of the initial entry level of achievement) together accounted for about 76 percent of the school variation in

Table 5–3
Summary of Multiple Regression Analyses Predicting Senior Test Scores
(Variance added)

Variable Entered into Regression Equation	Proportion of Test-Score Variance Explained	Increase in Variance Explained (percentage points)
Sophomore test	.722	72.2
Student-body attributes	.756	3.4*
School variables	.827	7.1*
Other student behavior	.836	.9*
Sophomore test	.722	72.2
School variables	.789	6.7*
Student-body attributes	.827	3.8*
Other student behavior	.836	.9*

* Statistically significant at the 0.05 probability level.

senior test scores. School variables accounted for an additional 7 percent of the total school variation. This suggests that schools do make a significant difference in student achievement; in contrast, student-body attributes account for only about an additional 4 percent of the differences among schools. It should be noted, however, that the level of achievement at entry (that is, test scores of sophomores) explains over 70 percent of the variance in the level of achievement at exit. This means that students' earlier level of achievement is greatly related to their subsequent achievement.

What Makes a School Different?

To answer this question, results of two types of analyses were used. The multiple regression analysis including the attributes of both school and student body was used to provide standardized regression coefficients that show the relative importance of each variable after all other variables in the model are considered. The results of this analysis are presented in Table 5–4. On the basis of the size of standardized regression coefficients, socioeconomic status and the percentage of black or Hispanic students in the school remain important predictors. Among school variables, the percentage of students in an academic curriculum stands out as the most important variable for predicting test scores. This is followed by the number of mathematics and science courses offered by the school and the school type. It is interesting to note that the regression coefficient for school type is positive, indicating that the test scores of seniors in public schools are higher than those of seniors in private schools after all other variables

Table 5–4
Standardized Multiple Regression Coefficients, Senior Cohort of 1980

Predictor Variables	Outcome Variables			
	Ed. Expect.	Absent.	Misbehavior	Senior test
Student-Body Attributes				
Average SES	.27*	.33*	−.04	.17*
Parental involvement	.00	−.06	−.04	.01
Parental press	.42*	.13*	.14*	.00
% black and Hispanic	.07*	.04	.14*	−.20*

School Variables				
School type (public)	−.11*	.09*	−.08	.08*
Competency requirements	−.03*	−.01	.00	.04*
School size	.10*	−.11*	−.12*	.01
Facility	.05*	.01	−.05	.02
Student-teacher ratio	.01	−.03	.03	.02
% teachers M.A., M.S., Ph.D.	.04*	−.09*	.08*	.00
Teacher turnover rate	−.05*	−.01	.08*	−.03
# mathematics, science courses	.03*	.09*	−.05	.10*
# other courses	−.01	.06	.09	−.02
Total hours in school year	.01	.05	−.07*	.03
Curriculum (academic)	.18*	−.20*	−.25*	.19*
Discipline rules	−.04*	−.05	.02	.05*
Effective discipline	−.08*	−.07*	−.17*	−.05*
Ability grouping	−.02	.02	−.01	−.02
Amount of homework	.08*	−.12*	−.13*	.02
Activity–intellectual	.06*	−.05	−.13*	−.01
Activity–artistic	.07*	−.08*	−.02	.07*
Activity–sport	.07*	.00	.04	.03
Activity–community	.01	−.01	−.06	.01
Student Behavior— Entry Measures (sophomore)				
Educational expectation	.02			
Absenteeism		.60*		
Misbehavior			.21*	
Sophomore test				.32*
Student Behavior— Outcome Measures (senior)				
Educational expectation				.22*
Absenteeism				.00
Misbehavior				.05*
Proportion of variance explained	.87*	.57*	.29*	.84*

* Statistically significant at the 0.05 probability level.

Table 5–5
Summary of Step-wise Multiple Regression Analysis Predicting Senior Test Scores

Variable Entered	Proportion of Test-Score Variance Explained	Increase in Variance Explained (percentage points)
Sophomore test scores	.722	72.2
Educational expectations	.779	5.7
Percentage of black or Hispanic students	.800	2.1
Mathematics and science courses	.808	.8
Academic curriculum	.816	.8
Socioeconomic status	.820	.4
Artistic activity	.823	.3
Effectiveness of school discipline	.827	.4
Misbehavior	.828	.1
Discipline rules	.830	.2
Minimum competency	.832	.2
Teacher turnover rate	.833	.1
Ability grouping	.834	.1
Sport activity	.835	.1

in the model are accounted for. Curricular program is also the strongest predictor for student behavior and educational expectations: schools that have higher proportions of students in the academic program have less student absenteeism and misbehavior, and their students tend to have higher educational expectations.

Results of stepwise multiple regression analysis also support the above findings. Stepwise multiple regression analysis was performed to identify variables that can add a significant contribution to predicting the test scores of seniors. In this analysis the variable accounting for the most variance was entered into the regression first, then the variable with the next highest contribution, and so on until further additions yielded no significant increase in predictive power. (This study used one-tenth of 1 percent of the school variance accounted for as the cutoff point; it is equivalent to about 0.5 point in test scores.) The results are shown in Table 5–5. Not surprisingly, the sophomore test scores are the best predictor of senior test scores, indicating that what students bring into school initially will greatly affect later outcomes. Socioeconomic status and the percentage of black or Hispanic students in the school remain in the model, indicating the importance of these student characteristics in predicting student achievement. Among school variables, curricular program and the number of mathematics and science courses offered in the school again show strong relationships to student achievement. Effectiveness of school discipline, artistic activity, minimum competency requirements, and discipline rules also show a slight relationship to student achievement.

CONCLUSION AND DISCUSSION

In summary, schools do make a difference. Certain types of schools are more likely than others to have students who behave well and score high on achievement tests. As shown by many previous studies, these schools tend to have students who come from families of higher socioeconomic status and whose parents are more involved in their education. What this indicates is that parents and home background play an important role in providing effective education to children. Although school administrators can do little to change a family's socioeconomic status, they certainly can encourage parents to take part in school activities. Inviting parents to meet with teachers and other school personnel, to observe classroom instruction, to discuss school curriculum, to participate in extracurricular activities, and to provide voluntary assistance to school and teachers, for example, will increase parents' awareness of school education, and, subsequently, parents will have proper expectations of their children's education. An effective school undoubtedly needs supportive parents.

An effective school also needs proper curriculum and practices. The results of the study show that regardless of student background, many school variables are related to higher student achievement. In particular, the number of science and mathematics courses offered, the total hours in the school year, and school discipline, as well as the proportion of students in academic programs, are significantly and positively related to student achievement. This means that schools that have orderly environments and offer an adequate academic curriculum will produce higher-achieving students. This study supports the recent educational reform movement to require a higher academic standard for high school graduation and to place a greater emphasis on school discipline as effective ways to increase student learning.

Other school variables that are related to higher student achievement include competency requirements and extracurricular activities. It is possible that the minimum competency requirement increases students' expectations of achievement as well as imposes pressure on students to study, and thus increases their achievement. The extracurricular activities that are offered in an orderly environment and attempt to enhance students' spirit for achieving excellence may also create a positive school climate conducive to higher achievement. School administrators and other policymakers should closely examine these activities.

A final note is that the effect of schools on student learning is at least as significant as the effect of parents. Schools are not merely the community extension of families; they can greatly enhance or supplement educational objectives of the community. The role of schools in achieving excellence in education will always be important, and should be duly respected.

Appendix 5–1
Specification of Variables

The variables used in this study are grouped in three categories: school variables, student-body attributes, and student outcome measures. They are specified as follows:

A. School variables: These were extracted from the school questionnaire file unless otherwise indicated.

1. *School type*: Public schools were coded 1, and private schools (mostly Catholic) were coded 0.

2. *Minimum competency requirements*: Whether seniors are required to pass a minimum competency (proficiency) test in order to receive a high school diploma. A value of 1 indicates presence of the requirement; a value of zero, its absence.

3. *School size*: Total number of students in grades ten and twelve.
4. *Quality of facilities*: Each of the following facilities, if present, contributed one point to a composite index of the quality of a school's facilities: indoor lounge for students, career information center, occupational-training center, media production facilities, remedial-reading center, departmental offices, teaching resources center for teachers, child or nursery care facilities, and student cafeteria.
5. *Student-staff ratio*: The ratio of the total school enrollment to the total number (or full-time equivalent) of school personnel, including student teachers, volunteers, security guards, and the like.
6. *Percentage of teachers with advanced degrees*: Percentage of the full-time high school teachers who have master's or doctor's degrees.
7. *Teacher turnover rate*: The percentage of full-time high school teachers in a school at the end of the 1978–1979 school year who had since left for reason other than death or retirement.
8. *Number of mathematics and science courses*: Total number of the following courses offered by the school: second-year algebra, calculus, chemistry, geometry, physics, trigonometry.
9. *Number of other courses*: The total number of the following courses offered in the school: auto mechanics, drama, driver training, economics, ethnic or black studies, family life or sex education, third-year Spanish, third-year German, third-year French, home economics, psychology, Russian, wood or machine shop. The figure can range from 0 to 13.
10. *Total hours in school year*: This was measured by the product of the following elements: number of days in a school year, duration of a standard class period (in hours), and the number of standard class periods the average student has each day.
11. *Academic curriculum:* The proportion of students in a school who reported themselves as enrolled in a college-preparatory (academic) program. A college-preparatory program (academic program) was coded 1; others, 0.
12. *Discipline rules:* Number of rules, from the following three, which are enforced in a school.
    a. Students responsible for property damage
    b. No-smoking rules
    c. Rules about student dress
    Scores can range from zero to three.
13. *Effectiveness and fairness of discipline*: Each student rated both the effectiveness and the fairness of discipline in his school, each on a four-point scale (1 = poor; 4 = excellent). The two ratings supplied

by each student were averaged. The mean of all the averages within a school was then calculated to yield a composite rating for each school. The data for these calculations were extracted from the student questionnaire file.

14. *Ability grouping*: Whether a school used homogenous ability grouping for either the tenth- or the twelfth-grade English classes. A value of 1 means that homogenous grouping was used, and 0, that it was not.

15. *Amount of homework*: Students were asked, Approximately what is the average amount of time you spend on homework a week? Values assigned to given response categories are as follows:

Values	*Response category*
0	No homework is ever assigned.
0	I have homework, but I don't do it.
1	Less than an hour a week.
2	Between one and three hours a week.
4	More than three hours, less than five hours a week.
7	Between five and ten hours a week.
10	More than ten hours a week.

16. *Participation in extracurricular activities*: Students indicated, on a three-point scale, the extent of their participation in each of a variety of extracurricular activities (0 = no participation, 1 = participation, and 2 = participation as a leader or officer). For purposes of this analysis, specific activities were grouped into four categories as indicated below. Scores of the activities of each student within each category were summed to provide an index of participation for that category. For each category, the index scores for all students from each school were then averaged to obtain a school index.

a. *Intellectual activities*
   (1) Honorary clubs
   (2) School newspaper
   (3) Subject-matter clubs
   (4) Student government

b. *Artistic activities*
   (1) Debating or drama
   (2) Band or orchestra
   (3) Chorus or dance

    c. *Sport activities*
      (1) Varsity sports
      (2) Other sports

    d. *Community activities*
      (1) Vocational education clubs
      (2) Community youth clubs
      (3) Church activities
      (4) Junior achievement

B. *Student-body attributes*
    1. *Socioeconomic status (SES)*: The SES index, which was based on student questionnaire data, is a composite of five equally weighted standardized components: father's education, mother's education, parental income, father's occupation, and a household items index. The SES index can have any value between approximately −3 to +3. Mean value is zero.
    2. *Parental involvement*: A measure of parents' involvement in their children's schooling was calculated from responses to certain items in the school questionnaire. The question was, To what extent is each of these matters a problem in your high school? (a) Parents' lack of interest in school matters and (b) Parents' lack of interest in students' progress. Each of these items had four response options ranging from "serious" (scored a value of 1) to "not to all" (scored 4). Responses to these two items were summed to yield a measure of parental involvement in each school. A high score indicates a high level of parental involvement.
    3. *Parental press*: This term refers to the amount of pressure that the parents in the school exert upon their children to get a good education. It was not measured directly. Each student's indication of the highest level of education that his mother wanted him to reach was taken as a proxy measure of parental press. The scores (years of schooling) ranged from 11 to 20 (11—less than high school graduation; 20—Ph.D, M.D., or other advanced degree).
    4. *Percentage of black or Hispanic students*: Percentage of students who are of Black or Hispanic origin, as reported by school administrators.

C. *Student performance*
    1. *Composite test score*: The average of standardized scores made by each student on the following tests: vocabulary, reading, and mathematics.

The mean of the standard scores was set at 50 and the standard deviation at 10. The reliability of the composite is about 0.90. The sophomores' scores and the seniors' scores were standardized separately.

2. *Absenteeism*: A simple average of three measures, each standardized to a mean of 50, with a standard deviation of 10. Sophomore and senior scores were standardized separately. The three measures are:
   a. Number of days absent from school for any reason other than illness.
   b. Number of days late to school.
   c. Whether or not the students reported cutting a class occasionally.

3. *Misbehavior*: A simple average of three measures, each standardized to a mean of 50, with a standard deviation of 10. Sophomore and senior scores were standardized separately. The three measures are:
   a. Have had disciplinary problems in school during the last year.
   b. Have been suspended or put on probation in school.
   c. Have been in serious trouble with the law.
   A higher score indicates a higher likehood of having behavioral problems.

4. *Educational expectations*: A student's own statement of the years of schooling he or she expected to obtain. The scaling is the same as that used for parental press.

REFERENCES

Averch, Harvey, et al. *How Effective Is School? A Critical Review and Synthesis of Research Findings*. Santa Monica, Calif.: Rand Corporation, 1972.

Bridge, R. Gary; Judd, Charles M.; and Moock, Peter R. *The Determinants of Educational Outcomes: The Impact of Families, Peers, Teachers, and Schools*. Cambridge, Mass.: Ballinger, 1979.

Brookover, William; Beady, Charles; Flood, Patricia; Schweitzer, John; and Wisenbaker, Joe. *School Social Systems and Student Achievement: Schools Can Make a Difference*. New York: Praeger, 1979.

Coleman, James A., et al. *Equality of Educational Opportunity*. Washington, D.C.: U.S. Government Printing Office, 1966.

Jencks, Christopher S., et al. *Inequality: A Reassessment of the Effect of Family and Schooling in America*. New York: Basic Books, 1973.

Jensen, Arthur R. "How Much Can We Boost IQ and Scholastic Achievement?" *Harvard Educational Review* 39 (Winter 1969): 1–123.

Madaus, George F.; Airasian, Peter W.; and Kellaghan, Thomas. *School Effectiveness: A Reassessment of the Evidence*. New York: McGraw-Hill, 1980.

Rutter, Michael; Maughan, Barbara; Mortimore, Peter; and Ouston, Janet. *Fifteen Thousand Hours: Secondary Schools and Their Effects on Children.* Cambridge, Mass.: Harvard University Press, 1979.

Takai, R. "Racial Difference in Cognitive Achievement." Paper presented at the meeting of the American Statistical Association, 1982.

Welch, Wayne W.; Anderson, Richard C.; and Harris, Linda J. "The Effects of Schooling on Mathematics Achievement." *American Educational Research Journal* 19, no. 1 (1982): 145–153.

6

Educational Research and Productivity

John R. Staver and Herbert J. Walberg

INTRODUCTION

Relationships between educational researchers and school administrators have had their ups and downs as each group communicates with the other. It is important to note, however, that each seeks the same goal—more effective teaching and learning in school. Differences arise, however, in the making of policy decisions that affect the quality of teaching and learning in schools. Researchers lament, in their less charitable moments, that administrators can see only the trees when the forest is plainly visible. Administrators complain, in equally less charitable moments, that researchers can see only numbers and statistics. Yet behind the numbers and statistics are human beings— children who attend schools.

It has been our experience that educational researchers must establish credibility with school administrators before the latter are willing to listen. Administrators expect researchers to see the children behind the statistics, to understand the practical problems of schools, and to relate the research of the ivory tower to the issues of education in the real world.

The root of the credibility issue seems imbedded in a characteristic bias of each group. The bias of the researcher is to be logical, to theorize, to hypothesize, to test empirically, to discover cause-effect relationships. Educational administrators also seek cause-effect relationships, but they do so in a more intuitive manner, especially in the face of sometimes ill-advised recommendations made by researchers on the foundation of their educational research findings.

The sometimes absurd recommendations of researchers—absurd at least from practical, fiscal, and political viewpoints—might be made because educational research lacks theories as powerful as those of the natural sciences. Scientific research has yielded theories of special and general relativity in physics, evolution in biology, plate tectonics in geology, and the periodicity of elements in chemistry. Yet we, as educational researchers, are at a loss to name an educational theory with similar power. And is it unreasonable for the administrator to use common sense, intuition, and whatever means are available in the absence of powerful explanatory theories in education? We think not. But we also think that research in education is the underprivileged great-grandchild of research in the natural sciences. For example, Glass (1972) has pointed out that in 1968 research in education totally or partially supported by public and private funds amounted to 2,000 person-years. In the same year, agricultural productivity studies were conducted by 15,000 full-time researchers, and 60,000 workers were involved in research and development in the health sciences. The axiom that one gets what one pays for clearly applies. Stephens (1967) declared, after reviewing several decades of research, that most educational techniques seem to hinder learning as often as they aid it.

In the years since Stephens's observation, the axiom concerning payment and results continues to be upheld. Three public organizations—the U.S. Office of Education, the National Institute of Education, and the National Science Foundation—together with other public and private agencies, have increased the funding of educational research. The results of their dollar contributions can be seen in substantial advances in our knowledge of teaching and learning. Our purpose in this chapter is to summarize recent research on teaching, learning, and educational productivity and to explore its implications for schools. In order to make decisions that will lead to more effective teaching and learning and greater productivity, administrators need to be aware of what recent educational research has to say regarding the improvement of teaching and learning.

RECENT RESEARCH REVIEWS

Walberg, Schiller, and Haertel (1979) compiled research reviews published from 1969 to 1979 of research on instruction and learning conducted in elementary, secondary, and higher learning institutions. The research reviews were listed in the *Current Index to Journals in Education* under the headings "Literature Reviews" and "State of the Art." The American Educational Research Association's *Review of Educational Research* and *Review of Research in Education*, plus other reviews, are cited in these sources. Also selected were forthcoming works that criticized and evaluated at least four studies. Most of the research was conducted in classrooms rather than under artificial conditions in laboratories. Because the reviews discuss the results of several studies, including comparisons within studies, it was necessary to supply a consistent framework for discussion. Studies are described in terms of the total number of results (positive and negative) and the percentage of positive findings. Positive is interpreted as support for the superiority of the techniques or conditions under investigation. The findings, presented in the aforementioned framework, are shown in Table 6–1.

Table 6–1 shows several impressive research results. Many findings support what can be described as "commonsense" decisions, whereas other results present food for thought, reflection, and change. Common sense tells us that increased time spent on tasks yields better performance on tasks. The twenty-five studies on time spent on learning clearly show a positive relation between time on task and achievement.

Class size has long been an important learning variable and the subject of intense negotiations between teachers' organizations and school districts. The findings exhibited in Table 6–1 reveal positive learning benefits for small classes. The credibility of these results is enhanced by the fact that the stronger studies show more favorable effects. Glass and Smith have done extensive work in this area. Their analyses show that in true experiments involving random assignment of students to small or large classes, the positive benefits of smaller over larger classes are increased. Random assignment negates the effects of other variables (for example, community wealth) on learning. Whereas the relation between class size and learning is by no

Table 6–1
A Selective Summary of a Decade of Educational Research

Research Topics	Number of Results	Percentage Positive
Time spent on learning	25	95.4
Innovative curricula on:		
innovative learning	45	97.8
traditional learning	14	35.7
Smaller classes on learning:		
pre-1954 studies	53	66.0
pre-1954 better studies	19	84.2
post-1954 studies	11	72.7
all comparisons	691	60.0
Behavioral instruction on learning	52	98.1
Personal systems of instruction on learning	103	93.2
Mastery learning	30	96.7
Student- vs. instructor-led discussion on:		
achievement	10	100.0
attitude	11	100.0
Factual vs. conceptual questions on		
achievement	4	100.0
Specific teaching traits on achievement:		
clarity	7	100.0
flexibility	4	100.0
enthusiasm	5	100.0
task orientation	7	85.7
use of students' ideas	8	87.5
indirectness	6	83.3
structuring	3	100.0
sparing criticism	17	70.6
Psychological incentives and engagement:		
teacher cues to student	10	100.0
teacher reinforcement of student	16	87.5
teacher engagement of class in lesson	6	100.0
individual student engagement in lesson	15	100.0
Open vs. traditional education on:		
achievement	26	54.8
creativity	12	100.0

self-concept	17	88.2
attitude toward school	25	92.0
curiosity	6	100.0
self-determination	7	85.7
independence	19	94.7
freedom from anxiety	8	37.5
cooperation	6	100.0
Programmed instruction on learning	57	80.7
Adjunct questions on learning:		
after text on recall	38	97.4
after text on transfer	35	74.3
before text on recall	13	76.9
before text on transfer	17	23.5
Advance organizers on learning	32	37.5
Analytic revision of instruction on		
achievement	4	100.0
Direct instruction on achievement	4	100.0
Lecture vs. discussion on:		
achievement	16	68.8
retention	7	100.0
attitudes	8	86.0
Student- vs. instructor-centered		
discussion on:		
achievement	7	57.1
understanding	6	83.3
attitude	22	100.0
Factual vs. conceptual questions on		
achievement	4	100.0
Social-psychological climate and		
learning:		
cohesiveness	17	85.7
satisfaction	17	100.0
difficulty	16	86.7
formality	17	64.7
goal direction	15	73.3
democracy	14	84.6
environment	15	85.7
speed	14	53.8
diversity	14	30.8

continued on p. 114

Table 6–1, *continued*

Research Topics	Number of Results	Percentage Positive
competition	9	66.7
friction	17	0.0
cliqueness	13	8.3
apathy	15	14.3
disorganization	17	6.3
favoritism	13	10.0
Motivation and learning	232	97.8
Social class and learning	620	97.6
Home environment on:		
verbal achievement	30	100.0
math achievement	22	100.0
intelligence	20	100.0
reading gains	6	100.0
ability	8	100.0

means the strongest or most consistent of the relationships summarized here, estimates from the work of Glass and Smith are most impressive. In a class of forty, students who average an increase of 1.0 grade equivalents each year would gain an average of 1.3 grade equivalents in a class of twenty. Thus, the average gain for students taught in classes of twenty from kindergarten through grade six is two years more than similar students taught in classes of forty for the same grades.

Mastery learning is a technique that has been implemented in both secondary and elementary schools. Its characteristics include clear goals and methods for small segments of learning, objectives stated in performance terms, formative evaluation by means of corrective feedback on progress, flexible learning time for learning units, alternative modes of instruction, and peer interaction in the learning process. Mastery learning is set apart from more conventional didactic methods in that it assumes that each student can achieve a minimum acceptable level, or mastery, given sufficient time. Table 6–1 reveals that on measures of achievement, retention, and attitudes, students who learn by mastery methods consistently outperform students who learn by conventional methods .

Programmed instruction has also found its way into the elementary and secondary schools. During programmed instruction, small elements of what is to be learned are presented in small units called frames. Students are active learners in each frame of well-designed programmed instruction. The length of the frame can be modified to fit the differing capabilities of students. A frame may be only a few sentences, a brief paragraph, or several pages. In this way, learners may quickly move through familiar material, branch to specific corrective segments, and learn at their own pace. The numbers presented in Table 6–1 show more favorable effects for programmed instruction than for conventional methods. The effects include both achievement and interest in the subject learned.

Several entries in Table 6–1 can be listed under a more general heading: "mathemagenic." This word was invented by psychologists about twenty years ago and is derived from two Greek words: (1) *mathema*—learning and (2) *genic*—give birth to. Specific instructional materials, content structuring, or teaching strategies may be examples of mathemagenic learning methods in the way they encourage or give birth to learning. Adjunct questions, advance organizers, analytic revision of instruction, and direct instruction are specific examples.

Adjunct questions are interrogatives inserted in text material. Several variations are possible, including insertion of the questions before, during, or after text reading. Further, the difficulty of a question can require only recall, or it can require transfer learning. Students answer the adjunct questions as they encounter them in the text. Table 6–1 shows that recall of information is improved consistently when adjunct questions appear after reading passages. Transfer learning also appears to be benefited by similar placement. Adjunct questions placed before reading improve recall but not transfer learning.

An advance organizer is an introductory technique that builds a relation between new content and what the learner already knows. The importance of advance organizers stems from the well-known fact that prior knowledge—what the student already knows—accounts for the largest component of variance in new learning. An advance organizer must possess certain characteristics in relation to the material it organizes. The organizer should possess a higher level of abstraction, generality, and inclusiveness than its material, and it is selected to provide maximum explanation, integration, and interrelation of the new concepts. An advance organizer, for example, could be used to compare and contrast forms of government. The numbers presented in Table 6–1 indicate that research on advance organizers has produced inconsistent results regarding improved learning effectiveness.

Analytic revision of instruction describes a method of lesson development. Instructional objectives are coupled with trial-and-error revisions of methods and materials until the objectives are reached. For example, an elementary school teacher presents a lesson on addition with renaming followed by evaluation of student performance. Difficulties encountered by students are identified, the lesson is revised accordingly, and it is presented again. The analytical revision process continues until the objectives are achieved. Table 6–1 shows that four studies were conducted, and their results unanimously reveal the superiority of analytic revision of instruction over conventional methods.

Direct instruction is characterized by those methods the teacher uses to control the major aspects of instruction. This type of instruction usually centers on the content of achievement tests. The results of four studies indicate that compared to conventional methods, direct instruction produces better gains in achievement. Direct instruction and, to a lesser degree, analytic instruction may, however, amount to teaching the test. Thus, the utility of these methods in achieving broad, general learning goals should be viewed with caution.

Teacher behavior has long been a fertile area for educational researchers. Teacher characteristics such as clarity, flexibility, and enthusiasm are important in the teaching-learning process. Research results, as shown in Table 6–1, indicate that achievement is enhanced under teachers who are clear in their expectations, goals, and learning methods; who show flexibility in their own responses to students; who exhibit enthusiasm for the subject and their students; who possess a high degree of task orientation; who use students' ideas in leading the lesson; who try to elicit answers from students to questions rather than tell the answers; who communicate the purpose and organization of the lesson content by structuring comments; and who avoid excessive criticism. Psychological incentives and engagements are other teacher behaviors that affect student learning. Teacher behaviors that stimulate students and reinforce desirable student responses and that engage the class as well as individual students in the lesson show consistently superior results.

On a more general plane, the concept of open education and its comparison with traditional education has been the subject of numerous investigations. A general description of open education is humane, enriched classrooms in which students are given some autonomy to plan, in conjunction with the teacher, learning goals, pace, method, and evaluation (Walberg and Thomas 1972). Leaders in the open education movement were intent on going beyond conventional achievement test outcomes; thus, many were hesitant about conventional evaluations. Our summary of the reviews, however, indicates that the fears of open education leaders were largely unwarranted. Of 102 studies, 76 found no significant differences between open and traditional education. Slightly more than 50 percent of the investigations in which significant differences were discovered found open education superior on traditional achievement instruments.

When authentically implemented open and traditional education are compared on the intended goals of open education, such as improved creativity, self-concept, school attitudes, curiosity, and independence, the results consistently favor open education. These results are cause for reconsideration by those who have concluded, based on the well-known Bennett (1976) study, that open education has failed. The findings suggest that more than conventional achievement is involved in successful learning.

Table 6–1 shows fifteen components of the social-psychological climate of classrooms and learning that have been studied. The learning outcomes are cognitive, attitudinal, and behavioral in nature. Positive correlations are found between all three types of learning and the classes that students see as cohesive, satisfying, challenging, democratic, and containing materials and facilities necessary for learning. Negative correlations are observed when the classroom climate includes friction among students, emphasis on cliques within classes, apathy toward lessons, disorganization in content and methods, and favoritism toward certain students. Student motivation seems undoubtedly related to the climate in the classroom. The studies surveyed show nearly unanimously (97.8 percent) that the level of student motivation and the amount of learning that occurs are positively related.

Student motivation and classroom climate are not controlled

solely by teachers. The abilities, attitudes, and behaviors of children are also heavily influenced by the home environment. A consistent positive correlation exists for social class and parental stimulation in the home with achievement and ability. Of the two indices, parental stimulation and encouragement are by far the more valid predictors of achievement and abilities. Parental stimulation is strongly correlated with verbal achievement, moderately correlated with mathematical achievement and intelligence, and weakly correlated with spatial and reasoning abilities.

A THEORY OF EDUCATIONAL PRODUCTIVITY

Even greater depth and confidence in research on educational effects is provided in the results of more thorough, quantitative syntheses, as compared to the percentages listed in the previous section. Such quantitative syntheses usually contain explicit search-and-selection procedures that permit scientific replication.

Intensive studies by several researchers (for example, Walberg and Haertel 1980) have identified nine factors as possible correlates or causes of school learning within a psychological theory of educational productivity. The nine factors can be categorized into three groups: (1) student aptitudes; (2) instructional variables; and (3) environmental influences.

Factors included in student aptitude are (a) ability or prior achievement, assessed by typical standardized instruments; (b) development, characterized by chronological age or maturation stage; and (c) motivation, indicated by scores on personality tests or willingness to persevere intensively on learning tasks. Instructional variables are represented by (a) the amount of time students spend on learning and (b) the quality of learning experiences, including the curricular and psychological aspects. Environmental influences include (a) the home; (b) the classroom as a social group; (c) the peer group outside school; and (d) the use of time outside school, specifically the amount of leisure-time television viewing.

According to the theory, learning may be expressed as a mathematical function of the nine factors (Walberg 1981). However, a series of statements provides a more qualitative explication that better serves present purposes. First, positive change in any factor increases learning. Second, continued positive change in any factor while other factors remain constant produces diminishing marginal returns. Third, if any factor becomes minimized, little learning takes place. Fourth, factors may substitute or trade off for each other, at the expense of diminishing return rates.

The five factors that form the student aptitude and instructional variable categories are prominent in a number of educational models, including Bloom's, Bruner's, Carroll's, and Glaser's. In accordance with the four statements above, each factor appears necessary for school learning.

Identification of important factors is a critical, initial step in the improvement of school learning. The next step includes analyzing alterations of the factors with the intent of maximizing school learning.

Alteration of the aforementioned factors raises yet another question. Who possesses the power to make such changes? Educators must realize that they retain somewhat limited ability in this arena. The time that students spend on learning and the quality of instruction are elements substantially controlled by educators. Yet, even these aspects are not completely alterable by educators. Diverse economic, political, and social forces outside the school exert significant influence on time spent on learning and the quality of instruction. Other influences on these aspects are the length of the school day and the school year, graduation requirements, and the exclusion of certain subjects at particular levels of the curriculum.

Educators can exercise limited influence on the student attributes of ability and motivation. The greatest influence on achievement is prior learning, that is, what the student already knows. High-quality classroom instruction coupled with sizeable time allotments are tools available to educators. But much prior learning occurs outside school, as student ability and motivation are also influenced by parents, peer groups, and students themselves.

Three of the environmental factors—the home, the psychological climate of the classroom, and the peer group outside school—influence learning in two ways. First, parents who provide enduring affection and academic stimulation at home, classrooms that possess a favorable psychological climate, and peers who have an interest in learning directly influence student learning. Second, these factors affect learning indirectly by influencing ability, motivation, and responsiveness to instruction, which in turn influence learning.

Similar to other environmental factors, the fourth environmental factor—the amount of leisure time spent viewing television—affects learning. Students typically watch about thirty hours of television each week (Walberg 1983). Research indicates that about ten television viewing hours per week seems optimal for learning (Walberg and Shanahan 1983). Increased television viewing comes at the expense of homework and other educationally and developmentally constructive out-of-school activities.

The description of the productivity model, its factors, and the mechanisms for change suggest an important consequence. Educators are likely to have only limited success in their efforts to raise achievement if they attack the problem alone. A coordinated effort of educators, parents, and community leaders is necessary.

Table 6–2 presents a summary of research findings on the nine factors of the productivity model in relation to school learning. The results are described by correlations and effect sizes. Correlations are quantitative estimates of the degree of association between two variables. A value of $+1.0$ represents a perfect direct association. A value of 0.0 indicates complete independence or no association, and a value of -1.0 shows a perfect inverse association between two variables. Effect sizes are quantitative values that convey the magnitude of differences. Such differences are frequently between experimental and

Table 6–2
Correlations and Effect Sizes for Nine Factors in Relation to School Learning

Factor	Number of Studies	Results and Comment
Instruction		
Amount	31	Correlations range from 0.13 to 0.71 with a median of 0.40; partial correlations controlling for ability, socioeconomic status, and other variables range from 0.09 to 0.60, with a median of 0.35.

Quality	95	The mean of effect sizes for reinforcement in 39 studies is 1.17, suggesting a 38-point percentile advantage over control groups, although girls and students in special schools might be somewhat more benefited; the mean effect sizes for cues, participation, and corrective feedback in 54 studies is 0.97, suggesting a 33-point advantage. The mean effect size of similar variables in 18 science studies is 0.81.
Social-Psychological Environment		
Educational	12	On 19 outcomes, social-psychological climate variables added from 1 to 54 (median = 20%) to accountable variance in learning beyond ability and pretests; the signs and magnitudes of the correlations depend on specific scales, level of aggregation (classes and schools higher), nation, and grade level (later grades higher); but not on sample size, subject matter, domain of learning (cognitive, affective, or behavioral), or statistical adjustments for ability and pretests.
Home	18	Correlations of achievement, ability, and motivation with home support and stimulation range from 0.02 to 0.82, with a median of 0.37; multiple correlations range from 0.23 to 0.81, with a median of 0.44; studies of boys and girls and middle-class children in contrast to mixed groups show higher correlations (social-classes correlations in 100 studies, by contrast, have a median of 0.25). The median correlations for three studies of home environment and learning in science is 0.32.

control groups. The effect size is defined as the z-score of the experimental group mean referenced in the frequency distribution of the control group (Glass and Hopkins 1984). Thus, the effect-size value is expressed in standard deviation units about the mean of the control

Table 6–3
Rating of Nine Productivity Factors

| | Instruction | | Social-Psychological Environment | | | | Aptitude | | | |
	Amount	Quality	Class	Home	Media	Peer	Age Develop.	Ability	Motivation	Median
Research										
Quantity	−	+	0	+	0	0	0	+	0	0
Correlation	0	0	+	+	0	0	0	+	0	0
Measures	0	−	+	−	−	−	−	+	0	−
Theory	0	−	0	−	−	−	−	0	0	−
Casual Basis										
Plausible	+	+	0	0	0	0	0	+	+	0
Statistical	+	+	+	−	0	0	0	−	−	0
Experimental	0	+	+	−	−	0	0	0	−	0
Priority										
Research	+	+	+	+	+	0	−	0	+	+
Policy	+	+	+	+	+	0	−	−	0	+

Note: The positive ratings for research and its causal basis are intended to suggest relative sufficiency or strength; the negative ratings are intended to suggest relative inadequacy or weakness; and the zero ratings are intermediate. Positive ratings for priorities are intended to suggest high priorities.

group, which is 0.0. Such z-scores are easily transferred to percentile points of the normal distribution, in which the control group mean is the fiftieth percentile (see Glass and Hopkins 1984, table A, pp. 522–527).

Presented in Table 6–3 are summary ratings on the research, its causal bases, and priorities for implementation for the three sets of new productivity factors. Correlations with learning are highest for ability measures such as IQ and prior achievement and for the educationally stimulating, social-psychological climate of the home and classroom. The amount and quality of instruction and the student's age, motivation, and peer-group characteristics correlate moderately with learning. Less exposure to popular television programming and similar media correlates weakly with academic learning among school-age children. Although considerable evidence on the magnitude of correlations of the factors with learning has accumulated, much work remains to be done to achieve consensus on theoretical definitions of the factors as well as inexpensive, practical, and valid measures of several of them.

The causal direction of the correlations, moreover, is open to question. It seems plausible enough, as Table 6–3 indicates, that the amount and quality of instruction and the student's ability and motivation are direct causes of learning, but it is also reasonable to think that more learning leads to greater motivation and that motivated students can stimulate the teacher. Also, it is unclear whether the social-psychological factors influence learning directly or facilitate it indirectly by increasing motivation and the amount and quality of instruction, including self-instruction. Statistical controls for ability, social class, and related variables have reduced the causal uncertainty with respect to amount and quality of instruction and class morale. But experimental controls with strict random assignment of students to educational conditions are the most convincing. More experiments on amount of instruction, for example, would allow us to assess more confidently the extent of the direct, one-way effect of instructional time on learning rather than examinations of correlations between the two that are possibly inflated with reverse causation. Since many experiments have been conducted on the quality of instruction and classroom climate, one can be more assured of the causal basis of these factors.

CLOSING THOUGHTS

Educational researchers must maintain some skepticism about causal research in field settings, the productivity theory, and evidence in general, because doubt and empirical testing are integral aspects of scientific research. Whereas the causes may seem obvious, the research does not yet fully support the hypotheses. Similarly, medical researchers retain some doubt concerning the causal connection between cigarettes and lung cancer, notwithstanding statistical controls for social class, area pollution, and animal experiments. The bottom line is that we need more and better research on the nine factors.

Decision makers in schools, however, cannot afford the luxury of waiting for definitive results that would make decisions clearer. Each day they must face the challenge of increasing learning effectiveness and educational productivity. On the basis of the evidence, the statistical and experimental controls, and plausibility, it seems that improvements in the amount and quality of instruction, the educationally stimulating qualities of the social-psychological environments of the class and the home, and exposure to mass media are likely to increase both the effectiveness and productivity of learning. It is possible, for example, that doubling the time students actually concentrate on instruction and study might nearly double learning, and that improvements in instruction and morale, discussed in the references cited, might redouble it.

Agriculture, industry, and medicine made great strides in improving human welfare as doubts arose about traditional, natural, and mystical practices; as the measurement of results intensified; as experimental findings were replicated, accumulated, and synthesized; and as their theoretical and practical implications were forcefully implemented. Education is no less open to humanistic and scientific inquiry and no less a priority when about half the workers in modern nations are in knowledge industries. Although we need more and better educational research, available research now points the way more definitively than ever before toward improvements that seem likely to increase educational effectiveness and productivity.

REFERENCES

Bennett, Neville. *Teaching Styles and Pupil Progress.* Cambridge, Mass.: Harvard University Press, 1976.

Glass, Gene V. "The Wisdom of Scientific Inquiry." *Journal of Research in Science Teaching* 9, no. 1 (1972): 3–18.

Glass, Gene V, and Hopkins, Kenneth D. *Statistical Methods in Education and Psychology.* 2d ed. Englewood Cliffs, N.J.: Prentice-Hall, 1984.

Stephens, John M. *The Process of Schooling: A Psychological Examination.* New York: Holt, Rinehart and Winston, 1967.

Walberg, Herbert J. "A Psychological Theory of Educational Productivity." In *Psychology and Education: The State of the Union,* edited by Frank H. Farley and Neal J. Gordon. Berkeley, Calif.: McCutchan Publishing Corp., 1981.

Walberg, Herbert J. "What Makes Schooling Effective? A Synthesis and Critique of Three National Studies." *Contemporary Education Review* 1 (Spring 1983): 23–34.

Walberg, Herbert J., and Haertel, Edward H., guest editors. "Research Integration: The State of the Art." *Evaluation in Education* 4, no. 1 (1980): 1–142.

Walberg, Herbert J.; Schiller, Diane; and Haertel, Geneva D. "The Quiet Revolution in Educational Research." *Phi Delta Kappan* 61 (November 1979): 179–183.

Walberg, Herbert J., and Shanahan, Timothy. "High School Effects on Individual Students." *Educational Researcher* 12 (August/September 1983): 23–34.

Walberg, Herbert J., and Thomas, Susan C. "Open Education: An Operational Definition and Validation in Great Britain and United States." *American Educational Research Journal* 9, no. 3 (1972): 197–202.

III

Effective Leadership

7

Sources of Constraints and Opportunities for Discretion in the Principalship

R. Bruce McPherson and Robert L. Crowson

INTRODUCTION

The organizational thickets of constraint and discretion appear to be particularly tangled for school principals, who serve both as representatives of their school system and as advocates for their particular schools. Some rich evidence of this standing dilemma was provided in a mid-1970s survey of Chicago public school principals conducted by the *Chicago Tribune*. Working with the approval and support of the Chicago Principals' Association, Education Editor Casey Banas and colleague Michael Smith prepared a 46-item questionnaire, which they mailed to the homes of all 535 principals in the system. Some 87 percent of the principals responded, and the survey results were published in a series of articles.

The front-page banner headline of January 4, 1976, read: WE'RE TOOTHLESS TIGERS, SCHOOL PRINCIPALS SAY. Banas (1976a, p. 1) reported:

> In the middle of the many problems of Chicago's schools, the city's public school principals are uncertain over how much authority they have to deal with those problems.
>
> They face increasingly complex social problems spilling into their schools, teacher militancy, burgeoning paperwork requirements, community conflicts, and myriad other problems.

> Seven of every 10 principals say the top priority of the school system should be to give them more authority to carry out their mission.
>
> 'The Chicago principal is a toothless tiger,' one said. 'Every conceivable responsibility is placed on his shoulders, but he is not given sufficient authority to do the job.'

The principals complained of a growing lack of respect for their role, of the overpowering attention that they were forced to give to discipline matters, of the transformation of their role from that of an educator to that of a manager, of the problems emanating from the implementation of the union contract at the local school level, and of the unreasonable demands that they act as parent surrogates. Repeatedly the respondents made reference to their being caught in the middle of the system, pressed by conflicting expectations and demands from many directions. One principal summarized a point of view regarding the source of the most serious problems: "My enemy is not the teachers, students, or community. It is 228 North LaSalle Street." Like 110 Livingston Street in New York, or 21st Street and The Parkway in Philadelphia, 228 North LaSalle Street housed (at that time) the vast central-office bureaucracy of the Chicago Public Schools.

Four days later, what was front-page news had been relegated to the second section and the editorial page. There interested readers could find a column by Banas (1976b) with a quite different headline: 10 TOP-RATED PRINCIPALS SEE NO LACK OF AUTHORITY. Banas had turned his attention to awards that had been presented in the autumn of 1975 by the respected Citizens Schools Committee to the ten principals ranked by the organization as the most effective in Chicago. Banas raised an interesting question:

> I asked Mrs. Hanchen Rosenbacher, chairman of the selection committee, if these principals had anything in common.
>
> 'Yes,' she answered. 'They all believe they have enough authority. They are not waiting around for instructions and rules and regulations from the district office or from downtown.'

At first glance, the dilemma appears to be spelled out in the counterpoint between the two headlines. The majority of principals in the city were constrained by the system, rendered frustrated and ineffective by a multitude of pressures they could not control or use; in contrast, a modest number of their colleagues were not constrained by that same system. Obedience to the system yields constraint and ineffectiveness, while affiliation with the local school is associated with discretion and effectiveness.

Reality is vastly more complex, of course. In the first place, the principal can never escape the necessity of dual commitment to the school system and the local school. Appearances and protestations sometimes to the contrary, the principal must work both sides of the street. Furthermore, for some principals the most powerful constraints are found in the local school community, while the most interesting opportunities for discretion can be identified in the larger system. For instance, in the turbulent 1960s and early 1970s local groups of parents forced many unwilling urban principals to vacate their offices, sometimes in a context of impending violence, even as other principals used political contacts with central-office colleagues to obtain disproportionate allocations of the budget and of material resources. A second complication is that issues of constraint and discretion appear to be linked to personal predilection, almost regardless of objective institutional factors. That is, if two principals look at the same professional situation, one may feel frustrated and paralyzed while the other may take creative action. In measuring the boundaries of action, the principal tends to ask two repetitive questions: Which of these problems that seem to be in my way are real, and which are not, and how do I tell the difference between them? and, How willing am I to act, even when I think I can get things to fall my way? These questions will be of interest to us, too, as we examine in this chapter the sources of constraint and the opportunities for discretion in the principalship.

SOURCES OF CONSTRAINT

Perhaps it is fortunate that the ambition of some men and women to become principals is strong; had they prior knowledge of the constraints to be placed on their future actions, many might hesitate to become candidates. That ambition—to accept wider and more-complex responsibilities; to extend service beyond the confines of a single classroom; to obtain and wield more power; to advance one's own ideas about how a school should be organized and operated; to make more money—masks the avalanche of real and imagined difficulties that seems to be the lot of the principal. In the following sections we point to some of the constraints of the principalship that are associated with socialization to the role; with the principal's perception of the system and the community; and with the work settings of school, school system, and community.

Socialization to the Role

Constraints related to socialization to the role of principal stem from two major preservice sources—experience and training—and these restrictions are aggravated quickly by institutional demands.

It is virtually an axiom that principals have been teachers. This fact is dictated not only by tradition, but in most states by law. Sporadic attempts to identify men and women who have had other experiences and to place them in principalships have been unsuccessful, for the most part. Often, work as a teacher is the only adult employment that the prospective principal has known. Furthermore, in many situations the principal has been a teacher in the very school that he or she must lead, or in the case of city school districts, in the system to which a primary commitment has been made. There are cosmopolitans as well as locals at the level of the principalship, but administrative mobility tends to increase with the second principalship or late in a career as the principal moves toward the central office and the superintendency. Reports have discussed the importance of teaching as a foundation for the principalship (Department of Elementary School Principals 1968; Meskin 1979). The general familiarity with the workings of a school that a principal gained while teaching is useful, and those principals who manage to include supervision and curriculum development responsibilities as central to their work understand the ethos of the classroom, which can both help and hinder them as administrators. But there is another side of the coin. Sarason (1971) points out that the teacher has had experience leading groups of children, but not groups of adults, and yet it is this second task that is much more critical for the principal. In addition, the teacher is essentially a loner, a solo performer behind the closed door of the classroom, whereas the principal must constantly interact with a stream of adults and children, often outside the confines of the office (Peterson 1977–78; Morris, Crowson, Hurwitz, and Porter-Gehrie 1984). Even more important is the fact that the average teacher sees only snapshots of the principal at work and develops only a scattered set of impressions of what principals actually do. Teachers usually assume that what they do not see is vastly more significant than what they do see, and this both is and is not the case. Having been a teacher (particularly at the elementary level) may provide one with a base for working in the areas of supervision and curriculum development, but working in a classroom often fails to ready an individual for leadership and management responsibilities. Consequently, socialization through experience is a mixed blessing for the new principal.

The relationship between professional education in school administration and performance as a principal may be even more tenuous than that between teaching experience and the principal's tasks. Bridges (1979) found that "most studies show no relationship between educational training and subsequent success in the principalship as judged by superiors and subordinates." Even when measures of acquired technical knowledge and skills or assessments of preparation programs by principals themselves are considered, Bridges contends that this basic pattern appears to hold true. In most states, a teacher can obtain a principal's certificate by presenting evidence of several years of teaching experience and by completing a master's degree in school administration in an approved university program. But if a teacher has a master's degree already in hand, let us say in the area of reading, the certificate typically can be obtained upon the completion of five "bottom-line" courses at a university: school administration; supervision; the school principalship; school finance or school law; and an internship or practicum. As important as these courses may be, it is difficult to imagine that they represent an adequate classroom and clinical exposure for an aspiring administrator. These lenient postures of state officials are designed with a maximum of deference for the wisdom and autonomy of university faculties and in response to the political pressures exerted by those same universities.

One looks in vain at standard certification requirements (as one would at the detailed curriculum in the universities) for required exposure to some of these realities in the life of a principal: problem-solving and decision-making processes and strategies; analysis of group behavior; policy and contract implementation; leadership behavior, with emphasis on issues of control, cooperation, and responsibility; understanding of the school and school system as organizations; formal planning; community relations and public information; time management; the translation of research findings for use by teachers; program and student evaluation; and group and individual testing. Furthermore, what is meant by clinical experiences? Are they on-site study of principals at work? Experience in completing administrative tasks in collaboration with a principal? Identification and solution of administrative problems on one's own authority and responsibility? Are some or all of these requisite? Who will decide?

This casual approach to administrator training has been challenged in some states by a vigorous new set of initiatives. In Illinois, for example, reform legislation in 1985 under Senate Bill 730 required administrative recertification every five years and indicated to university professors that all new certificate holders would need demonstrable knowledge related to productive parent-school relationships, and effective school climate, sound classroom organization, and instructional leadership. In Illinois, not just school districts but *schools* (and, of course, their principals) are to be held accountable. Principals are to begin doing forcefully and systematically that which has been extremely difficult in our profession—dismissing ineffective teachers. Furthermore, school districts are to submit "school report cards" to the general public, letting one and all know how each school shapes up against statewide and local standards. In addition to worrying about "the board," the principal now must worry about "the legislature." Constraint continues to expand in the political environment of local principals.

The liabilities of experience and training are complicated rather quickly by the demands of the institution as the teacher steps into the role of principal. The individual is suddenly part of management rather than of labor, one of the governors rather than the governed, and in many schools this separation is enforced by a union contract. In essence, the new principal is placed in an adversarial position with those whose cooperation is needed in determining the fate of the school and its children. This isolation is not complete, however, because teachers need principals for certain things. Gertrude McPherson (1979) has expressed their ambivalence eloquently:

What the teacher is saying to the principal, then, is: "Leave me alone. Don't interfere in my classroom. Don't tell me how to teach. Protect me from all who challenge me. Support my decisions. *And* show you care about and appreciate me." (P. 241)

The somewhat unexpected and typically unwelcome position of "friendly enemy" or "necessary adversary" is underlined by additional institutional realities. Reporting from a nationwide sample of principals in a variety of school and community settings, Salley, McPherson, and Baehr (1979) observed that organizational variables seem to be more powerful than socioeconomic or personal variables in differentiating job descriptions created by principals. They suggest that

personality can become an important factor after organizational constraints are understood, and it seems likely that increased relief from organizational constraints will permit the individual personality of the principal to have greater effects in the school setting. (P. 35)

Seemingly the principal must pay organizational dues first. At least initially, the size of the system and the size of the school will have a good deal more to say about how the principal spends his or her days than will the accumulated experience of the principal or the particular personality and ideas of the principal.

Curiously, the emphasis of the school reform movement fails almost completely to recognize the organizational dynamics of the principal-teacher relationship. Reformers are telling principals to play out energetically, even bullishly, an "instructional leadership" role that maximizes classroom observation time and the administrator's responsibility to evaluate teachers. In reality, principals have been reluctant to intrude too heavily upon teachers in their classrooms, recognizing that they need the cooperation of their teachers if the school is to remain in harmony. Some interesting data support this point. A study in Dade County, Florida, in 1964 provided the basis for Lortie's famous book, *Schoolteacher* (1975). This research was replicated in 1984—with comparisons in the responses of teachers over the twenty-year interim. A finding of special interest is that teachers were *less likely* in 1984 than in 1964 to say that they receive instructional help from their principals. Conversely, the teachers saw their principals as better overall managers of their schools in 1984, and they reported that they now receive more help from principals on discipline problems (Kottkamp, Provenzo, Jr., and Cohn 1986).

As excited as the new principal may be to sit in the principal's chair, to be in a position to really make a difference, he or she rather quickly has a sense of the walls closing in. Teachers' expectations and the expectations for school reform may not be in synch. Almost immediately, a new principal feels partially alienated from his or her teaching colleagues. The loneliness of the classroom is mediated by the friendship of teachers in the school, but in many schools the principal is the only administrator. A new network must be created or found with others who lead schools, and they are not very handy for impromptu conversations. Students, parents, and occasionally professional colleagues tell teachers how they are doing, but when a teacher becomes principal, the sources of praise and criticism seem much more uncertain and ominous.

If the new principal thinks at all about his or her preparation program at the university, it is usually with a sense of incredulity about its haphazard fit with this new and spinning world of the practicing administrator. As the days and weeks swirl by, principals are constantly reminded of their acquisition of responsibility and also of their loss of control. It is what others want you to do that seems to determine what you must do, and those others are often people you do not meet face to face. The ideas that filled the mental notebook and that seemed so easy to unfurl have now begun to appear fragile and even dangerous. Thus principals are thrown back at the beginning of their work on personal rather than on professional resources. Slowing down begins to make more and more sense. The teacher is told not to smile until Christmas of the first year, but the principal is advised to avoid making any major changes for an entire year.

The Perception of the System

The principal perceives school-system constraints in two basic ways. The first consists of viewing system-related problems one by one. The second involves seeing the system itself as the inchoate but pervasive constraint against which the principal must pit his or her skills and wit. We draw the reader's attention to this second configuration, the one that Sarason (1971) described from his contacts with urban school system inhabitants:

> The dominant impression one gains is that school personnel believe that there is *a* system, that it is run by somebody or some bodies in some central place, that it tends to operate as a never-ending source of obstacles to those within the system, that a major goal of the individual is to protect himself against the baleful influences of the system, and that any one individual has and can have no effect on the system *qua* system. There is no doubt in anyone's mind that the system "works" in the sense that children are in school, teachers teach, administrators administer—everyone is doing something for or with someone else—but rarely does one meet someone who believes it is working well and that his own job could not be done better if the system operated differently. (P. 133)

Surely this is the essential view of the Chicago Public Schools that the vast majority of its principals had in mind when they answered the questionnaires distributed by the *Chicago Tribune*. It is hardly a pretty picture to have tucked away in one's mind every working day and restless night.

Systems differ greatly, of course, with respect to size and style of operation. Sarason's description of a city school district would not portray a medium-size, suburban district. However, except in the smallest district, no single administrator can "see" and understand the whole system. This is certainly true for the principal (and is often the case for the superintendent). Inevitably it is the perception of the unknown and unclear aspects of the system that becomes the most frustrating and misleading constraint on the thought and action of the principal. And as much as principals try to learn about the system over the course of a contract or a career, they remain undereducated and miseducated.

Academic inquiries into the nature of the system of school district organization have given us three rather different models to consider. Rogers (1968) studied the New York public schools and painted a picture of refined, twentieth-century bureaucracy. He found local school principals at the mercy of a highly centralized staff at the 110 Livingston Street headquarters in Brooklyn, bound up by a system of rules and procedures and organizational offices that hampered their ability to manage and lead their schools. This analysis seemed a natural and accurate outgrowth of earlier studies and paradigms that supported a closed, bureaucratic understanding of school systems. Less than a decade later Weick (1976) characterized school systems as partially and significantly irrational. He did not see local schools and their principals as controlled completely by central and district offices and administrators. Moreover, "loose coupling" in the school system includes events and processes, such as planning, where intention and action are somewhat casually related. Weick's theory seemed to offer new explanations for the persistence of effective schools in deteriorating systems and for other local school adaptations and mutations. Meyer and Rowan (1978) a bit later tried to persuade us that large educational organizations exhibit features of both bureaucratization and loose coupling, the former with respect to the ritual classification of curricula, students, and teachers, and the latter with regard to instructional activities and outcomes. That is, both the Rogers and the Weick position may be correct. A contemporary study of Chicago principals by Morris and colleagues (1984) described the interplay between the central-office bureaucracy and decoupled schools in much more detail than earlier observational research related to the principalship (Wolcott 1973; Peterson 1977–78) and revealed much wider parameters for the discretionary behavior of principals than had been documented previously.

Principals have perceptions about the school system related to outcomes (or potency) as well as to structures and processes. We are reminded of this by the debate between Wirt (1980) and Miller (1981). Wirt, representing the liberal stance, argued that schools have had and will continue to have great effects on their students. Miller, acknowledging the neoconservative position, suggested that while schools do have such effects, we overestimate their impact and, in doing so, imagine that schools can do more for children and youth than they really can. Coleman I told us that schools did not count for as much as family, home, and community factors, but Coleman II suggested that schools, whether public or private, really do make a difference (Ravitch 1981). Following one or the other of these two basic positions makes a substantial difference in the professional life of a principal, particularly with respect to the patience and ingenuity he or she is willing to employ.

In all likelihood, scholars are beginning to discover what principals (and other practicing administrators) have known for a long time. The typical school system is both rational and irrational, a Rube Goldberg bureaucracy that works as it is supposed to just some of the time, replete with opportunities for the local school principal to play it by the book and by the seat of the pants. School systems are castigated for being overbureaucratized (too much red tape, ponderous, top-heavy) and for being underbureaucratized (fragmented, loose, even anarchic). While amenable to administrative control, they are also out of control. While replete with job descriptions, formal channels of communication, and officers reporting to other officers, they also have many mysterious, hard-to-fathom, and behind-the-scenes ways of *really* getting the work done. Rules and regulations are less instructive than one's own understanding and appreciation of the organizational culture—a developing feeling about how the system really works (McPherson, Crowson, and Pitner 1986). A principal develops a dominant set of feelings about the school system, and Sarason (1971) believes that it is this conception that shapes role performance, regardless of the accuracy of that conception. The system tolerates considerable variation in performance, and yet if the local principal does not establish his or her own locus of control, the system appears to be monolithic and accepting of a somewhat narrow range of behavior.

The average principal, like the average sergeant, grumbles but complies. Control is exerted in the school on behalf of the system. Responsibility is defined in terms of allegiance to the system first and to the school second. Cooperation is measured by employee compliance with system policies, programs, and values. Initiative is a dirty word. The less typical principal may grumble as much, but he or she certainly complies less. Control is exerted in the school on behalf of the school. Responsibility is defined in terms of allegiance to the school first and to the system second. Cooperation is measured by collective values, plans, and actions in the school and school community. Initiative is the order of the day. Naturally, the system as Goliath makes it difficult for principals who lean in this direction. They had best be clever.

Both types of principals develop a working view of the system. The average principal is—by nature and experience—acquiescent, managerial, and concerned with policy delivery. The less typical principal is—by nature and experience—competitive, entrepreneurial, and concerned with service delivery. Personality fuses with training and professional experience to produce such predilections. Real constraints cannot be ignored, are not subject to bluff or finesse, draw the spotlight of attention, and may have harmful short- or long-term effects for the principal and the school. Captive of the system or not, the principal must deal with these problems. Tragically, some principals do not treat the system seriously and do not see the system as either monolithic, disjointed, or even eclectic in its composure, but rather as unreal. These principals tend to ignore the system and its constraints. They are crushed and discarded as administrators because they have failed to play the game by one of the two fundamental sets of rules.

Constraints in the School, System, and Community

If a principal's perceptions of the administrative role lead to a collection of hindrances, a parallel set of institutional and community-based expectations confound the picture. The conventional wisdom of the principalship (a composite view of what the building principal *should* do) suggests that the principal serves first and foremost as the "instructional leader" of the local school. The principal is expected to devote by far the largest portion of his or her day to the direct supervision of instruction, to staff development, and to other activities that provide an effective "learning environment" for students. A bit further down the scale of values are expectations that the principal will plan and implement change; effectively manage the increasingly complex school; and mediate relationships between the school system and its surrounding publics. These various expectations constitute the *professed goals* of the typical educational organization. As Perrow (1978) has observed, however, there may be counterposed against the professed goals an equally salient set of *operative goals*— based upon some very different kinds of institutionalized expectations. An organization's operative goals are no less "real" or important than its stated objectives; in fact, they may often assume central importance. An organization's operative goals may speak, for example, to such needs as (a) maintaining employment (plus the provision of current resources and benefits) for the work force, (b) promoting the overall stability of the organization, (c) maintaining good relations with "key" interest groups, and (d) regulating the behavior of potentially "deviant" persons within and even occasionally outside the organizations (Boyd and Crowson 1981). Cronin has repeatedly observed that he and his colleagues did not really begin to understand the Boston public schools until they realized that the school system served first and foremost as a bastion of protected professional employment. Thus, a number of expectations surrounding the school principalship speak to objectives well beyond the stated, commonly recognized ends of school administration. The building principal (no less than the district superintendent) finds himself or herself faced with some institutionalized needs for survival, political fence-mending, job stability—needs that further define (and constrain) the nature of the administrative job.

As the managerial official in closest contact with education's key clientele (pupils and parents), the principal has been labled a "street-level bureaucrat" (Lipsky 1976, 1980) and a "boundary-spanner" (Moore 1975), with recognition in each case that the school-site level of administrative responsibility is central to the all-important task of translating policy into practice. Although at the lowest level of administrative officialdom, the building principal establishes and redefines a good deal of educational policy while supposedly just "carrying it out." A central source of constraint upon the principalship, while implementing school-system policy, is a need to balance, to pursue simultaneously, and sometimes to make choices between the organization's professed goals and its operative goals. In counterpoint with the expectations for instructional leadership, for example, is the well-ingrained, widely accepted norm of teacher autonomy. Despite their responsibilities for classroom observation and control, principals conform heavily to the ideas that "My job is to free teachers to teach" and "My job is to back my teachers up." The result, frequently, is not unlike the example of one principal, who expressed dismay and disbelief ("Oh, that couldn't have happened") in hearing from a parent that her fourth-grader's teacher had been hitting some of the pupils with a ruler. Afterwards, in private, the principal exclaimed: "I've warned her before to put that ruler down."

Similarly, despite an avowed press for an openly reciprocal relationship with parents and the community, the building principal is expected in reality to play a key role in helping the school system avoid environmental uncertainty. Considerable pressure for site-level stabilization comes from hierarchical superiors (Morris et al. 1984), who generally expect a local principal to keep his own ship in order, to manage localized conflict without troubling the upper bureaucracy.

This phenomenon has been observed in a number of studies of the principalship and has been variously labeled as an organizational press for "variety-reducing behavior" and "keeping the lid on" (Wolcott 1973); "good order" and "efficient housekeeping" (Sarason 1971); and "keeping things calm" (Blumberg and Greenfield 1980). Principals will try to "co-opt" dissident parents, to "socialize" outsiders into organizationally acceptable patterns of behavior, to control or "cover up" events that begin to get out of hand, and to urge (sometimes bully) parents into conformity with the school's categorizations of pupils and services (Crowson and Porter-Gehrie 1980; Weatherley 1979).

Differences between the expectations of hierarchical superiors and the demands of the school also infringe upon the principal in other ways. Kerchner, Mitchell, Pryor, and Erck (1980) studied implementation of the union contract by principals, and found them caught between a central-office demand for uniformity in the application of the contract and a need for flexibility in their own local schools as they adopted individual situations. A Chicago research team discovered that principals are engaged occasionally in a bit of "creative insubordination"—they will bend organizational rules in ways that serve school-system clients at the apparent expense of the larger bureaucracy. The building principal may ignore or even disobey orders from above in order to dilute their dehumanizing effects (Morris et al., 1984, pp. 143–149).

As a last point, we note with Meyer and Rowan (1978) that a central dimension of what is operative in an organization is its effort to maintain a prevailing belief system, a set of mystifications or mythologies that help to define the profession. One of these is Willower and colleagues' (1973) observation that a "pupil-control ideology" reigns supreme in school management. Despite a press for innovation and change, we find the building principalship in reality heavily involved in the maintenance of decorum, disciplinary order, and stability (Martin and Willower 1981; Morris et al. 1984). Like policemen on the beat, building administrators make sure that they are most conspicuously visible during time of heavy student traffic, "trouble spots" are closely watched, and the school's groups of most consistently unruly youngsters are frequently checked. Frequent hall tours typically are used to convey additional messages of proper student behavior and attire, plus a sense of orderliness and school cleanliness. Time spent in this fashion becomes, of course, a constraint of some magnitude in the midst of a busy day filled with many other expectations; relatively little time is left for the thinking and planning that would accompany the professed objectives of leadership or change.

OPPORTUNITIES FOR DISCRETION

Our discussion now turns to principals' opportunities for discretion in their work. We believe that even as there are real and formidable constraints, there are also real and powerful opportunities for discretionary behavior in the principalship available to principals who become comfortable with the scope of the role, who can handle problems effectively, and who can identify and maintain sufficient and meaningful work incentives.

The Scope of the Role

The role of principal is a cluttered one. As Wayson (1979) has observed, the principal is required to figure out how to "own" the role under the press of myriad and often contradictory demands. The role is malleable, and this is what the principal can discover after coming to grips with organizational constraints and developing a posture toward the system itself. We see that role as associated with three primary tasks—the exercise of responsibility, the maintenance of control, and the development of cooperation—and thus composed of three overlapping role components—teacher, manager, and leader.

The teacher has been responsible for a classroom and a certain number of students, but a principal is responsible for a school and many teachers, classrooms, and students. The transition from focused to diffuse responsibility is a difficult one for most principals, and often the new principal will assume too many burdens of accountability. The prowling and exploring behavior of principals in the school building and on its grounds represents one version of the anxiety over responsibility. In the process of learning how to handle more responsibility, the typical principal has diminished one aspect of it that should be pivotal—the responsibility to teach.

The principal must capitalize on his or her teaching experience rather than permit it to assume the form of a liability. Teaching other adults how to function more effectively in the school community (and often in ways the principal sees as desirable) is part of the principal's job, but one that is often unfulfilled. People cannot be expected to know or do what they have not experienced or been taught. Ideally the school should be as much a learning community for adults as it is for children. In addition to working as a teacher of adults, the principal's responsibility to teach should include at least instructing a small group of students on a regular basis. Acceptance of this phase of responsibility, and performing such teaching functions, sets the stage for the principal really giving leadership to the instructional program, perhaps in the categories of activity identified by Edmonds (1979). But when the principal is not a teacher, when the principal has divorced himself or herself from the formerly central activity, then the principal will spend time completing management tasks at the expense of instructional tasks. We believe that the principal's responsibility to teach should be a cornerstone of the role.

A good deal of the minutiae that end up on the principal's desk distract the principal from exercising significant control over the school. Familiarity with certain matters in complete detail is required of the principal, to be sure, particularly as such understanding is related to leadership performance. But repetitive and mundane management details must be delegated, rejected, or ignored. What the principal should be concerned with controlling are decisions and allocations within four key areas—the reputation of the school; the rewards for performance; the physical, professional, and instructional resources; and the agenda of ideas that animates intellectual exchange within the school community. While these foci mirror to a certain extent what is happening and what is possible in the larger system, they must be applied to the school first. The school secretary can complete reports and manage the financial books, but she cannot argue with the superintendent over the need for classroom renovation or debate with the PTA president over what should be discussed at all-school meetings. And as much as the principal must be concerned with the reputation of the school system, the best way of ensuring the improvement of that reputation is through the control and enhancement of the reputation of the *school*.

Leadership in a school is not much different than it is in any organization of similar size and complexity. Success or failure of leadership is measured by the capacity of the principal to persuade people to do certain things, both singly and collectively, for the good of the school. The principal as leader obtains this cooperation chiefly by helping to clarify the goals and expectations of the school; through organization; by hiring individuals and placing them in certain locations within the organization; and by stimulating communication among individuals in the various roles in the organization (Barnard 1938). The smart principal seeks people who will cooperate with one another rather than simply with him or her. Cooperation persists beyond the tenure of the particular principal, and as it is expressed in a school it represents an accumulation of the effects of past leaders and shared leadership. The principal who obtains additional cooperation has made contact with both the past and the future of the school.

We have urged here a view of the scope of the principal's role that includes a responsibility for teaching; managerial control over the reputation, rewards, resources, and idea agenda of the school; and leadership in developing cooperation through goal clarification, personnel assignment, and communications building. What might we expect to find in preservice professional preparation programs for the principalship related to this set of ideas? First, the continuity between teaching and administrative experience would be emphasized, and a larger share of courses would be related to curriculum development and supervision, to the assessment of individual and group instructional outcomes, and to adult education. Special instruction would be focused on the structuring of role and the maintenance of role priorities, and in this effort distinctions would be drawn between what it is that principals tend to do and what it is that principals ought to be doing. However, the major revision would be in the area of clinical experiences. An understanding of the major tasks and role components of the principalship requires deliberate, clear, staged, and extended exposure of the aspirant to the role being performed both as it typically is and as it should be. We can envision an internship composed of three periods—study of the role through the use of ethnographic techniques; work in collaboration with a principal; and work in completion of assigned tasks under the more general supervision of a principal. The easing of the neophyte into the exercise of responsibility, control, and leadership should closely parallel the pattern established for medical doctors in training (Schwab 1964).

The nature of the principal's role is as vulnerable to shaping as is its scope. Some principals probably heed the chapter headings of a recent publication of the National Association of Secondary School Principals titled *Principals: What They Do and Who They Are* (Weldy 1979). Lined up, they pose an assertive picture of life in the principal's office: "An Authority Figure," "An Educational Leader," "A Decision Maker," "An Acknowledged Expert," "A Problem Solver," and "A Disciplinarian." But compare that list to the words a group of outstanding principals from suburban school districts gave one of the authors when asked to identify the single word that best described the principalship as they knew it: authenticity, flexibility, listening, facilitating, learning, juggling, caring, and waiting. Both the power and the capacity to govern educators is shifting from the central office to the school and from the principal's office to the classroom. A role for the professionalization of education takes place. Here system discretion will lead to personal discretion; the molding of the principal's role in the future may well depend more on nuance and influence than on direction and control.

Using the Problem Cycle

As he was helping to put together the initial issue of the *New Republic*, Walter Lippmann wrote to his old mentor, Graham Wallas, in England: "I begin to see somewhat more clearly why administrators have not time to think, and why people who think often can't administer" (Steel 1981, p. 74). Lippmann's remark is amusing but somewhat too facile, at least with respect to school principals. They have time to think about many of their problems; what they must decide, and often in a matter of a few seconds, is how long they should think before acting. Faced with an enormous number of problems, they cannot devote a good deal of reflective thinking to each problem. Yet for those most difficult problems, who is to say that extended reflection is dysfunctional? Lippmann's extremes actually reveal both sides of the administrator as problem solver—reactive and reflective in a variable pattern, dispatching some problems quickly and holding onto others for extended periods of time.

We have trained administrators for the schools to have faith in a problem-solving process that begins with a given problem and then moves through distinct stages: the identification of alternatives, typically through a review of personal and institutional experience and through the seeking of advice; the selection of the "best" alternative; action by the administrator and others; and, finally, a period of reaction. Yet the problem is not always given, and if it is given, it is not always accepted by the administrator. The thought that precedes action, that helps define the problem is not always given, and if it is given, it is not always accepted by the administrator. This thought, which fills out the complete problem cycle, is termed *problem finding*.

It is the dynamic relationship between the dilemma and the problem that defines problem finding. By dilemma we mean quite simply a perplexing, puzzling situation that attracts the attention of a human being. Ominous clouds on the horizon are of as much interest to the family driving toward the picnic grounds as they are to the pilot about to fly in the direction of the potential storm. The issue is hardly one that can be avoided—should the family drive back home for the safety of the kitchen? Should the plane be wheeled back into the hangar? Like most dilemmas, the storm is not something that people can work with easily. They must wrest from the dilemma a problem that is manageable and understandable and, above all else, potentially amenable to solution. If the family knows that there is a large shelter on the picnic grounds, their problem may take a particular form. In turn, if the pilot senses that the weather hides a tornado, then his problem may take a quite different shape. In these cases, or hundreds and thousands of others, it is this tension between an unclear dilemma and the possibility of a well-defined problem that sets the stage for problem finding.

Some of the intellectual roots of problem finding can be found in the writings of the American pragmatic philosophers, such as Charles Peirce and George Herbert Mead and most especially John Dewey. Dewey's analysis of reflective thinking provided a crisp description of the phenomenon. He specified five phases of reflective thinking, which compose what we might call the problem cycle, ranging from problem finding through problem solving:

(1) *suggestions*, in which the mind leaps forward to a possible solution; (2) an intellectualization of the difficulty or perplexity that has been *felt* (directly experienced) into a *problem* to be solved, a question for which the answer must be sought; (3) the use of one suggestion after another as a leading idea, or hypothesis, to initiate and guide observation and other operations in collection of factual material; (4) the mental elaboration of the idea or supposition as an idea or supposition (reasoning, in the sense in which reasoning is part, not the whole, of inference); and (5) testing the hypothesis by overt or imaginative action. (Dewey 1933, p. 107)

We are drawn particularly to Dewey's first two phases of problem finding. He points out in the first of these that the mind is suggesting and testing possible solutions even before the problem is completely formulated. In the second, movement from the dilemma to the problem occurs. What has been emotional is intellectualized, and problem solving may begin. Dewey is not intrigued with "ready-made problems," which he dismisses as assigned tasks, but rather with those situations where a dilemma clouds a problem (or problems) for an individual.

Hanson (1979) completed research in California schools that gives us interesting glimpses of administrative problem finding and solving. He found that the initial inclination of administrators was to avoid dealing with problems altogether. Other gate-keeping strategies included claims of "no jurisdiction"; talking a problem to death; stalling; sustained ignoring; and reinforcement of others' (for example, teachers') resistance to a problem. Problems tended to penetrate these screens when tension persisted; under crisis conditions; when cloaked as central-office directives; when maneuvered through human "soft spots"; and when a screen was removed voluntarily by administrators.

In addition to *accepting* or *rejecting* dilemmas and problems, the mature principal has several other modes of problem finding at his or her disposal. Sometimes principals must be clever in *discovering* problems—in finding the "real" problem that is hidden behind the preferred problem. Another mode involves *initiating* behavior, and it includes those occasions when the principal is the actual source of the dilemma, or when the principal frames problems that challenge the thinking of others. Predicting can help to find problems, and it occurs when a principal looks to the future and raises dilemmas or problems that do not require immediate attention but have a shaping effect on the school and school community.

If principals are to influence their roles and the problem agendas of their schools, they need to become as consciously involved in problem finding as they are in problem solving—working across the full problem cycle with ease and control. That is, the functions of teacher, manager, and leader (as we have defined them) are extended by problem finding and problem solving. Dewey (1938, p. 108) stated the matter bluntly: "A problem well put is half solved." Getzels (1979), too, has recognized that problem finding involves selection and consequently command of the attention and energy of organizational participants:

> The world is, of course, teeming with dilemmas. But the dilemmas do not present themselves as *problems* capable of resolution or even sensible contemplation. They must be posed and formulated in fruitful and often radical ways if they are to be moved toward solution. The way the problem is posed is the way the dilemma will be resolved. (P. 5)

Framed one way, a problem will keep a school on its present course. Framed another way, a problem will move a school in a quite different direction, perhaps toward radical change.

Understanding and Using the Incentive System

Regardless of how a training program is organized or how goals are specified or how jobs are defined, people at work will tend to behave in response to the reward structure they face. Not infrequently, an organization's incentive system is much better adapted to the attainment of its operative rather than of its professed goals. Thus, both teachers and principal may emphasize crisis prevention, organizational stability, and "good soldiering" in their school environments rather than risk taking, problem finding, or programmatic creativity. They do so because getting ahead in the system has been generally recognized as a function of demonstrated ability in smoothing troubled waters rather than roiling them.

Not uncommonly an organization's incentive system will contain gaps where neither professed nor operative goals appear to be maximized. Morris and colleagues (1984) found, the example, that building principals tend to shape their jobs to suit their own performance preferences:

> . . .like other workers, principals hold attitudes toward their own role; they like some parts of the job and dislike other parts, and they shape the job. Principals will spend time doing that which they most enjoy, think they are good at, or believe will most likely 'make a difference.' Other aspects of the job or of the expected and normative role are not much emphasized.

The research team found principals, for example, redefining the supervisory role—spending little time in classroom observation and much time doing things that appeared to relate in some way to the supervisory role expectation but had a better chance for some payoff, for an end product. Principals were also observed emphasizing work they believed they did well and deemphasizing whatever failed to satisfy them.

The organizational incentive system, additionally, may produce outcomes that place educational goals in conflict. Both Rogers (1968) and Morris and colleagues (1984) report instances where a formula-based (using pupil enrollment levels) procedure for ensuring an equitable and efficient allocation of resources to individual schools fostered a reluctance on the part of principals to transfer any of their students for purposes of desegregation.

We have failed to train school administrators to understand the reward system that surrounds them. Indeed, little scholarly attention has been given to this topic. Beyond the insightful work of Lortie (1969) and beyond some nuggets to be gleaned from a few "classics" in the sociology of education (for example, Waller 1932; Bidwell 1965), there has been little investigation into the organizational incentives in education. Yet, research at the University of Chicago suggests that even the pedagogical decisions teachers make within classrooms are tied to higher administrative decisions in the distribution of resources and rewards (Ferguson 1979–80).

From the perspective of the educational organization, top-level administrators need to know many things about how persons at lower levels (for example, principals and teachers) are likely to react (given the incentive structure) in the face of policy initiatives. Will principals actively pursue meaningful parental advisory committee involvement in their schools if an operative objective of the organization (well wrapped in promotion opportunities) is to keep the press of community interests and expectations at bay? Can a voluntary, open-enrollment plan for school-district desegregation succeed within a system that allocates all resources to school buildings (including the size of principals' salaries) on the basis of student enrollment levels? Can principals be expected to respond with dispatch to a request for information from a "downtown" office whose head is known to be currently out of favor with the system's general superintendent?

From the perspective of the principal, there is a great deal to be learned not only about the place of the building administrator within the reward system of the larger organization, but also about the managerially creative, discretionary use of incentives within the school as well. Principals who know and understand their opportunities for discretion will recognize the many rewards that are available in meeting employee welfare needs, employee advancement interests, freedom-to-do-the-job concerns, and employee recognition needs.

Time spent, for example, in shaking missing checks out of a downtown payroll office, assisting teachers in obtaining corrections in payment (for example, getting paid for the correct number of disability leave days), and covering for teachers who need a day off (beyond the number of personal leave days that are usually permitted)—are just a few of the *welfare* actions of the principal. Of course "cooperative" and "productive" teachers are likely to receive much more attention and assistance than those considered "goof-offs" or "troublemakers."

Similarly, and as mentioned previously, we find the building principal critically involved in the socialization of employees into the norms and standards of the profession. While there are many classroom teachers, there are relatively few chances, proportionately, for *advancement* into positions of higher status and remuneration. This narrow funneling of upward mobility places much power in the hands of the building principal. The initial identification of, assistance to, and experiential training provided to persons with advancement potential rest typically with a principal who first takes an interest in and brings someone along.

Paralleling the limited-advancement characteristic of the profession is Lortie's (1969) observation that an intrinsic system of rewards to teachers exerts a powerful hold upon the profession. Teachers turn inward, to their classrooms and to their pupils, and receive much satisfaction from working with students. Both teachers and principals soon discover, however, that the autonomy (*freedom-to-teach*) norm creates much dependency. Teachers count on principals to control the intrusion of unruly pupils and parents into the classroom order, to ensure a necessary flow of instructional materials and supplies, to coordinate school activities in such a way as to minimize classroom interruptions, and to absolve teachers from as many nonteaching responsibilities (such as playground patrol, paperwork) as possible. Again, principals find that some teachers usually deserve more assistance and autonomy than others.

Finally, although intrinsic rewards are of compelling value, the profession's limited opportunities for status differentiation and teacher *recognition* give the principal another useful managerial tool. Teachers no less than their pupils respond with pride to the display of their students' work on school bulletin boards. Morris and colleagues (1984) report that twice each year (in January and in June) one of their subjects (a high school principal) awards ribbons and certificates to his faculty with the fewest absences. Although there is much joking and kidding at the awards ceremony, the recipients pinned their ribbons on immediately and continued wearing them.

CONCLUSIONS

We have suggested that the role of school principal is characterized by a tantalizing web of managerial constraint and discretionary opportunity. Some principals appear to be heavily burdened by the "boundedness" of their jobs, while others award themselves managerial freedoms that extend far beyond what the system supposedly will allow. Although the experiential, institutional, and political forces influencing principals are often similar, the personal predilections and perceptions of individuals regarding the limits of what *can* be done appear to vary considerably.

Three central categories of constraint upon the principalship are the forces associated with (a) socialization to the role; (b) perceptions of the system and the community; and (c) the congeries of expectations flowing from the work settings of school, the school system, and the community. In counterpoint, three categories of discretionary opportunity for principals are (a) the broad scope of the managerial role, (b) the many opportunities for a creative use of the organizational "problem cycle," and (c) education's reward structure.

The process of socialization from teacher to principal provides a poor adaptation, overall, to the reality of the job. The principal is thrust from labor directly into management; from the camaraderie of one among many to the isolation of one, alone; from a job that looks inward at children into a role that must look inward but also outward (toward parents and the community) and upward (toward the rest of the educational organization). For many, the walls close in, the problems overwhelm, the role becomes a lonely burden of responsibility without leverage, of delegated authority without control. The socialization process has failed to engender an appreciation of the malleability of the role, of the opportunities for a creative structuring of the job (using control over the reputation, rewards, resources, and idea agenda of the school), and the opportunities for a stimulating continuity between teaching and the administrative experience. School systems are bureaucratic and predictable; anarchic and irrational; command-oriented and politicized; inward-directed and paranoid. Those who perceive all of this complexity as opportunity rather than as constraint are able to shape performance that rises above anarchy toward control, that becomes entrepreneurial rather than complacent. These persons appear to be few in number. Some who do succeed are problem finders rather than merely problem solvers (or worse, problem ignorers). They are intrigued by a dilemma, a perplexing or puzzling situation. They think, they initiate behavior, and they look to the future. Dilemma or constraint becomes *problem*, something capable of resolution and managerial control.

In the final analysis, a successful principalship requires an answer to the question: How willing am I to act? Despite some formidable constraints, a principal can act. There are many opportunities for the creative use of intiative, for the discovery of problems out of dilemmas, and for the development of control out of confusion.

REFERENCES

Banas, Casey. "We're 'Toothless Tigers,' School Principals Say." *Chicago Tribune*, 4 January 1976. (a)

Banas, Casey. "10 Top-Rated Principals See No Lack of Authority." *Chicago Tribune*, 8 January 1976. (b)

Barnard, Chester I. *The Functions of the Executive*. Cambridge, Mass.: Harvard University Press, 1938.

Bidwell, Charles E. "The School as a Formal Organization." In *Handbook of Organizations*, edited by James G. March. Chicago, Ill.: Rand McNally, 1965.

Blumberg, Arthur, and Greenfield, William. *The Effective Principal: Perspective on School Leadership*. Boston, Mass.: Allyn and Bacon, 1980.

Boyd, William L., and Crowson, Robert L. "The Changing Conception and Practice of Public School Administration." In *Review of Research in Education*, vol. 9, edited by David C. Berliner. Washington, D.C.: American Educational Research Association, 1981.

Bridges, Edwin M. "The Principalship as a Career." In *The Principal in Metropolitan Schools*, edited by Donald A. Erickson and Theodore Reller. Berkeley, Calif.: McCutchan Publishing Corp., 1979.

Crowson, Robert L., and Porter-Gehrie, Cynthia. "The Discretionary Behavior of Principals in Large-city Schools." *Educational Administration Quarterly* 16 (Winter 1980): 45–69.

Department of Elementary School Principals. *The Elementary School Principalship in 1968*. Washington, D.C.: Department of Elementary School Principals, National Education Association, 1968.

Dewey, John. *How We Think: A Restatement of the Relation of Reflective Thinking to the Educative Process*. Boston: D. C. Heath, 1933.

Dewey, John. *Logic: The Theory of Inquiry*. New York: Henry Holt, 1938.

Edmonds, Ronald R. "Some Schools Work and More Can." *Social Policy* 9, no. 5 (1979): 28–32.

Ferguson, Teresa L. "Using a Multilevel Framework to Examine Variations in Grouping and Instructional Format Patterns." *Administrator's Notebook* 28, no. 3 (1979–80): 1–4.

Getzels, Jacob W. "Problem Finding and Research in Educational Administration." In *Problem Finding in Educational Administration*, edited by Glenn L. Immegart and William L. Boyd. Lexington, Mass.: D. C. Heath, 1979.

Hanson, Mark E. *Educational Administration and Organizational Behavior*. Boston: Allyn and Bacon, 1979.

Kerchner, Charles T.; Mitchell, Douglas; Pryor, Gabrielle; and Erck, Wayne. *Labor Relations and the Muddling of School Governance*. Claremont, Calif.: Labor Relations Research Project, Claremont Graduate School, 1980.

Kottkamp, Robert B.; Provenzo, Eugene F., Jr.; and Cohn, Marilyn. "Stability and Change in a Profession: Two Decades of Teacher Attitudes, 1964–1984." *Phi Delta Kappan* 67 (April 1986): 559–567.

Lipsky, Michael. "Toward a Theory of Street-Level Bureaucracy." In *Theoretical Perspectives on Urban Politics*, edited by Willis D. Hawley et al. Englewood Cliffs, N.J.: Prentice-Hall, 1976.

Lipsky, Michael. *Street-Level Bureaucracy: Dilemmas of the Individual in Public Services*. New York: Basic Books, 1980.

Lortie, Dan. "The Balance of Control and Autonomy in Elementary School Teaching." In *The Semi-Professions and Their Organization*, edited by Amitai Etzioni. New York: Free Press, 1969.

Lortie, Dan. *Schoolteacher: A Sociological Study.* Chicago, Ill.: University of Chicago Press, 1975.

Martin, William T., and Willower, Donald J. "The Managerial Behavior of High School Principals." *Educational Administration Quarterly* 17 (Winter 1981): 69–90.

McPherson, Gertrude. "What Principals Should Know about Teachers." In *The Principal in Metropolitan Schools,* edited by Donald A. Erickson and Theodore L. Reller. Berkeley, Calif.: McCutchan Publishing Corp., 1979.

McPherson, R. Bruce; Crowson, Robert L.; and Pitner, Nancy J. *Managing Uncertainty: Administrative Theory and Practice in Education.* Columbus, Ohio: Charles E. Merrill Publishing Co., 1986.

Meskin, Joan D, "Women as Principals: Their Performance as Educational Administrators." In *The Principal in Metropolitan Schools,* edited by Donald A. Erickson and Theodore L. Reller. Berkeley, Calif.: McCutchan Publishing Corp., 1979.

Meyer, John W., and Rowan, Brian. "The Structure of Educational Organizations." In *Environments and Organizations;* edited by Marshall W. Meyer and associates. San Francisco, Calif.: Jossey-Bass, 1978.

Miller, Harry L. "Pollyanna in the Policy Patch: A Response to Frederick Wirt." *Educational Evaluation and Policy Analysis* 3, no. 5 (1981): 83–93.

Moore, Mary T. "The Boundary Spanning Role of the Urban School Principal." Ph.D. dissertation, University of California, Los Angeles, 1975.

Morris, Van Cleve; Crowson, Robert L.; Hurwitz, Emanuel, Jr.; and Porter-Gehrie, Cynthia. *Principals in Action: The Reality of Managing Schools.* Columbus, Ohio: Charles E. Merrill Publishing Co., 1984.

Perrow, Charles. "Demystifying Organizations." In *The Management of Human Services,* edited by Rosemary C. Sarri and Yeheskil Hasenfeld. New York: Columbia University Press, 1978.

Peterson, Kent. "The Principal's Tasks." *Administrator's Notebook* 26, no. 8 (1977–78) 1–4.

Ravitch, Diane. "The Meaning of the New Coleman Report." *Phi Delta Kappan* 62 (June 1981): 718–720.

Rogers, David. *110 Livingston Street.* New York: Vintage Books, 1968.

Salley, Columbus; McPherson, R. Bruce; and Baehr, Melaney. "What Principals Do: A Preliminary Occupational Analysis." In *The Principal in Metropolitan Schools,* edited by Donald A. Erickson and Theodore L. Reller. Berkeley, Calif.: McCutchan Publishing Corp., 1979.

Sarason, Seymour. *The Culture of the School and the Problem of Change.* Boston: Allyn and Bacon, 1971.

Schwab, Joseph J. "The Professorship in Educational Administration: Theory-Art-Practice." In *The Professorship in Educational Administration,* edited by Luvern L. Cunningham. Columbus, Ohio: University Council for Educational Administration, 1964.

Steel, Ronald. *Walter Lippmann and the American Century.* New York: Vintage Books, 1981.

Waller, Willard W. *The Sociology of Teaching.* New York: Wiley, 1932.

Wayson, William W. "A View of the Leadership Shortage in School Buildings." In *The Principal in Metropolitan Schools*, edited by Donald A. Erickson and Theodore L. Reller. Berkeley, Calif.: McCutchan Publishing Corp., 1979.

Weatherley, Richard A. *Reforming Special Education: Policy Implementation from State Level to Street Level*. Cambridge, Mass.: MIT Press, 1979.

Weick, Karl E. "Educational Organizations as Loosely Coupled Systems." *Administrative Science Quarterly* 21 (March 1976): 1–19.

Weldy, Gilbert R. *Principals: What They Do and Who They Are*. Reston, Va.: National Association of Secondary School Principals, 1979.

Willower, Donald J.; Eidell, Terry L.; and Hoy, Wayne F. *The School and Pupil Control Ideology*. University Park: Pennsylvania State University, 1973.

Wirt, Frederick M. "Neoconservatism and National School Policy." *Educational Evaluation and Policy Analysis* 2, no. 6 (1980): 5–18.

Wolcott, Harry F. *The Man in the Principal's Office*. New York: Holt, Rinehart and Winston, 1973.

8

Triangulation of Selected Research on Principals' Effectiveness

Chad Ellett and Joseph Licata

Frances Vazquez became principal of Morris High, in the South Bronx, New York, in 1979. At that time, the school was known for violence, and students wandered the halls rather than attended classes. About the same time, Adan Salgado became principal of A.S. Johnston High in Austin, Texas, a school almost entirely composed of minority students whose academic achievement lagged behind that of virtually all other Austin high school students. "We were the doormat of the district," recalls Salgado. George Washington High in Los Angeles also got a new principal in 1979—George McKenna. McKenna's new assignment had similar problems: violence, absenteeism, and as Margaret Wright, a parent-group leader, recalled, "Morale was terrible, the rooms were dirty, and 90 percent of the teachers were rotten." Four years later, these schools and principals were noteworthy for other reasons—a report by the Ford Foundation claimed that these schools had much improved (Garcia 1983).

What made these schools improve? The central reason was thought to be the development of school pride stimulated by the energetic, sometimes outspoken leadership of these three principals. Their efforts seemed to mobilize students, teachers, parents, and community. According to Edward Meade of the Ford Foundation, "In some cases the motivation was as simple as, 'We were known as the lousiest school in town, and we don't want to be the lousiest school'." As a result, more students in these three schools have been doing home-work every night, taking more academically difficult courses, regu-larly attending classes, and seeking further education upon graduation (Garcia 1983).

Certainly, along with the work of the principal, school improve-ment and student achievement probably result from other important variables such as a supportive home environment, student motiva-tion, and effective teaching. These variables and selected others have been included in structuring educational productivity functions (Wal-berg 1978). Yet the notion that an effective principal plays an impor-tant role in making a positive difference in schools tends to reoccur in continuing discussions and research on schooling. Conventional wis-dom suggests that "good" schools and "good" principals go hand in hand. Garcia's (1983) report in *Time* magazine, noted above, is but one example of the literature supporting the importance of the effec-tiveness of principals as a variable in explaining effective or improved schools. Bossert, Dwyer, Rowan, and Lee (1983) recently provided a comprehensive framework and documentation for understanding the effectiveness of school principals as instructional leaders and man-agers. Recent, comprehensive reviews of research on effective schools provide additional documentation supporting the importance of the school principal in fostering positive school outcomes (Block 1983).

The purpose of this chapter is to explore four important research projects on the effectiveness of principals in order to identify several research propositions and theoretical insights derived from cross-checking findings and perspectives from these studies. Denzin (1970) suggests that the use of multiple data sources, multiple measures, multiple methodologies, and multiple theoretical orientations im-proves the validity of findings in social science research. To the extent that the results of multiple sources of evidence are congruent, the data and their interpretation are believed to be valid. The logic of this multi-operational, or *triangulation*, strategy suggests that, as in trigo-nometry, one can indirectly but accurately measure the location of a point through sightings from other points. In other words, all mea-sures, methodologies, and theoretical orientations have their own specific weaknesses, and by concentrating on a particular social phenomenon with a series of independent, indirect, and possibly weak indicators, researchers may minimize separate indicator error and maximize overall validity (Williamson, Karp, and Dalphin 1977). While this chapter is at best only a summary and analysis of four selected research projects that focus on the effectiveness of principals, the range of data sources, methodologies, and theoretical approaches provides an informal opportunity to triangulate or cross-check approaches and findings as a means to strengthen our insights.

No formal decision rules were employed in selecting these four studies. We selected them because they are fairly recent works, employ data sources and theoretical and methodological approaches, and together provide a wide enough range to make a rough triangulation of findings possible. The studies include a qualitative research project employing interviews of out-of-the-ordinary principals who reportedly make a positive difference in their schools (Blumberg and Greenfield 1980); a quantitative study exploring school-innovation efforts and principals' effectiveness (Miskel 1977); a competency-based research project presenting a comprehensive set of measures of principals' performance and the field test of a performance-validation paradigm (Ellett and Walberg 1979); and a quantitative test of hypotheses derived from contingency leadership theory employing multiple measures to investigate the job challenge of the principalship and the effectiveness of principals (Peregrine 1982).

THE FOUR STUDIES

Out-of-the-Ordinary Principals

Motivated by suggestions from colleagues, schoolteachers, administrators, and parents that exceptional, particularly effective principals were present in local schools, Blumberg and Greenfield (1980) selected eight of these allegedly out-of-the-ordinary principals for extensive interviewing. These principals were selected informally from reports of their reputation. Each was seen by researchers and by his or her colleagues as making a difference in the school. The eight included four elementary principals (three male and one female) and four secondary principals (two male and two female).

The methodology of this study was qualitative. While the researchers did use follow-up questions to clarify points, they conducted the interviews without an interview schedule, opting instead to allow these principals to present self-portraits. Once the interviews were completed and a manuscript drafted, six of the eight principals met with the investigators to give their reactions to the way they were portrayed and to discuss as a group what Levinson (1973) has called the "emotional toxicity," or strain, of their occupation. In the interviews and the final group meeting, principals' remarks were tape-recorded, transcribed, and later analyzed by the researchers as a means to gain insight about what makes these individuals different. Data were collected during the fall of 1975.

Referring to a study by Carroll (1978) of the central life interests of 277 principals, Blumberg and Greenfield (1980) noted that Carroll identified 17 percent of the sample as being job-oriented, 44 percent as non-job-oriented, and 39 percent as having no preference. They suggest that this 17 percent of job-oriented principals was not unlike the group they selected for interviewing. These principals, like Carroll's 17 percent, felt strongly that "the job was the thing."

Based on an analysis of interview data, the investigators were able to describe three factors that offer an explanation, at least in part, for the principals' effectiveness. First, they had a need and an eagerness to make their schools over in "their" image. This characteristic was called *vision*, that is, the principals had definite ideas about what they wanted their school to be like. Second, they appeared proactive and willing to take the initiative. This initiative involved careful listening and observing and having a keen sense of when to push, when to sit back, when to involve others, and when to be decisive and move ahead on one's own. Third, they were resourceful in structuring their roles and the demands on their time. They set their own agendas and moved toward the realization of their vision. While they satisfied routine maintenance demands, they did it in a way that reduced the possibility of their being tied down by second-order priorities.

Considering these notions about effective principals, defined as those substantially above the norm for effectiveness in their profession, Blumberg and Greenfield (1980) present a tentative theory for leading a school. Recalling Lewin's (1951) formula, Behavior = f(Person, Environment), the investigators suggest that understanding the behavior of their out-of-the-ordinary principals is a matter of understanding them as persons as well as understanding the structure and dynamics of the social system in which they act.

Schools, the researchers say, are part of a loosely tied network that links principals in an ambiguous way to other principals and central-office administrators. This results in a feeling of isolation in the principalship, which inevitably leads principals to turn their attention inward to their schools. Internally, the school is described as a setting of immediacy wherein demands are made on the principal by various members of the system. These demands frequently require immediate responses. The notion of ontological insecurity (Laing 1969) was applied in an institutional sense to characterize the school's uneasiness about its vague and diffuse goal structure and its public vulnerability. Blumberg and Greenfield (1980) suggest that the values of teachers and principals that stress a smooth-running operation and professional autonomy could inhibit collaboration, change, or leadership that makes a difference.

In this situation principals are seen as being confronted regularly by teacher norms that do not encourage collaboration. As a result, principals' efforts at change are directed more at individual teachers rather than at particular teachers' groups. Given this context, Blumberg and Greenfield (1980) conclude that it takes a very special type of principal to lead a school and make a difference. Their application of the $B = f(P,E)$ framework suggests that in the situations noted above, out-of-the-ordinary behavior by a principal can be expected only when the principal as a person (P) has certain needs. They summarize a description of these needs: (1) the need to take charge of a situation rather than be controlled by the situation itself or by others; (2) the need to include in decision making those who will be affected by the decision; and (3) the need to both express and receive friendliness, warmth, and good-natured fellowship.

Two years after their collection of the data, the investigators noted that four of the principals interviewed had left their position, three more were talking about a desire to leave, and only one seemed satisfied enough to continue. In their discussion of the emotional toxicity, or strain, of the job, the authors present three problem areas that these principals as a group saw as disturbing: (1) the tenure system and the difficulty in terminating a poor teacher; (2) the powerlessness they felt over certain matters both external and internal to the school; and (3) the expectation that principals should always be rational, which inhibits them from showing their emotions or "blowing off

steam." While these factors clearly add to the tension of the principalship, the authors speculate about tensions generated by special principals trying to make a difference—trying to collaborate when teacher
norms inhibit it; trying to give and receive warmth in an environment
emphasizing frequent, immediate decisions; trying to make changes
when smooth operation is valued. As Blumberg and Greenfield (1980)
note, referring to the seven who were dissatisfied or left the principalship, "It may be that there is a certain restlessness or a certain
wariness that accompanies being the sort of principal who makes a
difference in a school." Of course, principals who leave their positions
are not necessarily "good" principals.

Principals' Effectiveness and Innovation Efforts

The effectiveness of principals can be understood by noting the
perceptual evaluation by subordinates and superordinates and can be
influenced by situational factors like the interpersonal climate of the
school and the technology level of the school district. Further, numerous descriptions in the literature on the principalship often associate
effectiveness with the innovation efforts of the principal.

Miskel (1977) studied the relationships among these variables,
using a sample of 160 elementary and secondary principals selected
through stratified, random sampling of 39 large school districts in a
midwestern state. Eight teachers for each principal were sampled as
subordinates. As superordinates, the superintendent, assistant superintendent, or director of elementary and secondary education evaluated the principals in each district. Caplow's (1966) organizational
effectiveness framework, which delineates four essential organizational processes (stabilization, integration, voluntarism, and achievement), was used to develop a measure of innovation efforts. Five
open-ended questions asked teachers and principals to list recent
programs that had been initiated or maintained in relation to these
organizational effectiveness processes. The content of the responses
was analyzed for the number of different programs under each dimension. Telephone interviews with each principal verified each list of
innovations.

Two forms were developed to measure principals' effectiveness,
based on Wofford's (1971) research. Teachers completed a "subordi-

nate form" and central-office administrators completed a "superordinate form." The teachers' form asked for ratings on five items that complete the question, "How effective is the principal in . . .?" The five items included establishing order and appropriate procedures or setting specific goals and performance measures. A Likert-type scale with choices for answers ranging from "ineffective" to "very effective" was used to assign values to teachers' ratings. Ratings on the five items were summed to produce a score for each teacher. A sociometric, fixed-alternative interview schedule, which asked a central-office administrator to rate the most and least effective principals in each of the five areas, was used to produce a measure of the superordinates' ratings of principals' effectiveness. Alpha coefficients for each measure from the two forms were 0.80 and 0.83, respectively.

Miskel (1977) employed the *Situational Description Questionnaire* (SDQ) to measure teacher perceptions of the technology level of the school district and the interpersonal climate in the school building. The SDQ was adapted from a form developed by Baumgartel and Jeanpierre (1972) for use in industrial settings. The technology subscale includes items like, "Does your school district have organized programs for training and development of its administrators, group leaders, and teachers?" Interpersonal climate indicators included questions like, "How free and open are the interpersonal communications among administrators and teachers in your school?" Each subscale was composed of six items scored on a four-choice scale. Alpha coefficients were 0.69 for technology and 0.83 for interpersonal climate, respectively.

Miskel (1977) predicted significant main and interaction effects for the teachers' ratings of principals' technology level and the interpersonal climate on central-office administrators' ratings of the effectiveness of principals and innovation efforts. A similar prediction was made for central-office personnel's ratings of principals' effectiveness for the technology level and for the interpersonal climate on teachers' ratings of principals' effectiveness and innovation efforts. Miskel also predicted significant main and interaction effects for innovation effort, for technology level, and for interpersonal climate on teachers' and central-office administrators' ratings of principals' effectiveness.

However, analyses of the ratings found no significant interaction effects. All three performance variables—innovation efforts, superordinates' perceptions of principals' effectiveness and subordinates' perceptions of principals' effectiveness—were found to have reciprocal main effects. The main effects of situational variables on performance variables were derived in four out of twelve instances. The findings suggested that (1) a high technology level in the district is associated with school-building innovation efforts; (2) teachers' positive perceptions of their school's interpersonal climate are related to positive perceptions of the principal's effective performance; and (3) measures of principals' performance and type are directly related to each other.

Miskel (1977) concluded that these findings suggest a complex set of relationships involving innovation and may explain some of the difficulty principals experience in trying to initiate new programs. As a result, situational factors like the technology level of the school district and school climate might be taken into account in evaluating principals' effectiveness or innovation efforts. These considerations appeared to be important, not only for evaluation of principals, but for selection of principals as well. In cases where a principal has been previously effective in a relatively favorable situation, it may be important for those considering the principal for a new position to realize that past effectiveness may be related more to situational factors than to the actual "competence" of the principal.

Competency, Environment, and Outcomes

Ellett and Walberg (1979) present a performance-based theoretical framework describing the interactive relationships among principals' competency, the school environment, and student learning outcomes. The model is an extension of a performance-validation paradigm originally described by Payne, Ellett, Perkins, Klein, and Shellinberger (1975). The framework rests on the proposition that ". . . causal relationships, however complex, exist between principals' behaviors and key variables within the school environment." Their assumption is that principals' performance affects important dimensions of the school environment that mediate student learning outcomes, and that these outcomes, in turn, affect principals' future performance. Basic to this framework is the notion that the principal takes a role in a highly interactive social setting and is often affected by the results of his or her own behavior.

The Ellett and Walberg (1979) model is presented in Figure 8–1. Solid lines in the model represent the hypothesized impact of principals' performance on other variables. Broken lines symbolize the effects of the consequences of principals' behavior on their subsequent performance. These broken lines also represent internal and external environmental influences on principals' performance. Mediating the relationship between principals' behavior and student outcomes are factors associated with the cognitive, affective, and behavioral characteristics of individuals within the school environment (students and teachers) and outside the school environment (community members, parents, central-office administrators). Student attendance, learning, and subsequent achievement are considered student outcomes. The lines in the figure can be understood as various causal "paths" to be posited for describing principals' performance within the school environment.

Using as an example the causal path from 1 (principal) to 5 (the student), Ellett and Walberg (1979) suggest that the principal might perceive a situation in the school, develop an intention, and behave accordingly. The behavior might be in relation to any of the other variables, depending on the principal's initial perception and intent; or, the intended consequences of the act may be mediated by their immediate impact on others. One example Ellett and Walberg present to clarify this path involves a principal who perceives and responds to a student discipline problem with the intention of changing the student's behavior. They note that discussions with the student's teacher may affect the teacher's perception of, intentions for, and behavior toward the student and mediate the principal's original intent. Similarly, outside the school, the principal's interaction with the student's parents may affect the parents' perceptions of, intentions for, and behavior toward their child and mediate the principal's initial intent. The consequences of the principal's behavior or mediated intent, represented by the return paths (broken lines), may affect the principal's future perceptions, intentions, and behavior in similar discipline cases. Thus, the model describes a complex ebb and flow of causal relations between the behavior of principals, its consequences, and multiple school outcomes.

A field test of the basic relationships in this model was undertaken as part of a statewide project in Georgia to identify and validate

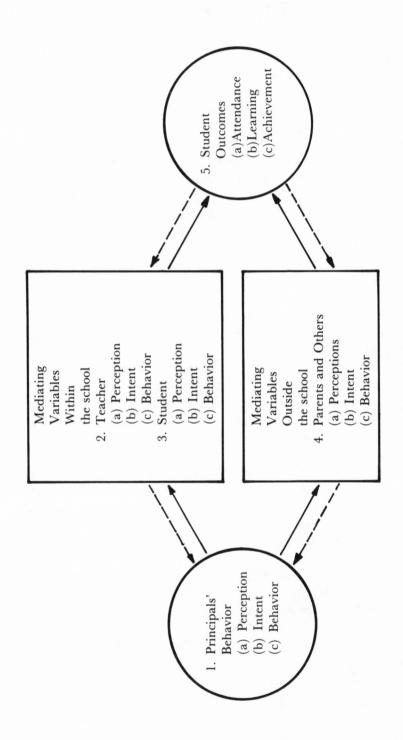

Figure 8-1

Interactive Model for Principals' Competency, the Environment, and Outcomes

performance competencies for public school principals. Project ROME (Results Oriented Management in Education) focused on the development of a system for assessing principals' performance and establishing the criterion-related validity of the system (Ellett 1976).

The ROME investigators developed an initial pool of 3,500 to 4,000 statements of competencies, duties, functions, and roles for school principals. These data were classified to produce 306 competency statements. To verify these statements, principals were polled statewide, which further reduced the list to a highly valued set of 80 performance statements perceived as important for the effective operation of a school. This list of 80 competencies was then operationalized by a system of 885 behavioral indicators. From interviews with principals, the investigators reduced these indicators to 338 performance indicators perceived by the principals as essential or highly desirable for the effective operation of a school.

Content analysis was used to assign each of the 338 verified performance indicators to appropriate assessment sources. For example, indicators of principals' performance in working with teachers on curriculum development were seen as appropriate for assessment by teachers. Assessment sources were the school principal, teachers, central-office personnel, students, and an external observer. Instrumentation was developed for each of these reference groups, using Likert-type ratings of the perceived frequency and effectiveness of the school principals' performances. The result was a relatively high-inference set of measures called the *Principal Performance Description Survey* (PPDS), which includes Principal, Student, Teacher, Central-Office, and External Observer Forms. These instruments have since been reduced in length and further refined (Ellett and Payne 1978).

The validation research measured, as mediating variables, teachers' and students' perceptions of characteristics of the school environment. Teachers' perceptions of their work environment were measured by the 118-item, 14-subscale *School Survey* (SS) (Coughlan 1970). Students' perceptions of characteristics of the school climate and of the learning environment were measured by either the 105-item, 15-subscale *Learning Environment Inventory* (LEI), appropriate for students in grades seven to twelve, or the *My School Inventory* (MSI). The MSI is a school-level adaptation of the *My School Class Inventory* (MCI) (Anderson 1973). The MSI consists of 45 items and 5 subscales and is appropriate for pupils in grades two to six. Subscales of the SS measure teachers' perceptions of work environment factors such as administrative practices, supervisory relations, colleague relations, educational effectiveness, professional and nonprofessional workload. The LEI and MSI measure pupils' perceptions of school climate factors such as cohesiveness, difficulty, apathy, satisfaction, democracy, goal direction, and diversity.

The School Survey was originally developed as a measure of teachers' morale or work satisfaction. Research with the SS in the Chicago Public Schools has shown that teachers in schools with the largest student achievement gains viewed their schools as being more effective and themselves us having more constructive supervisory relations with the principal, closer community contact, and a greater voice in educational programs than did teachers in schools with the lowest student achievement gains (Coughlan and Cooke 1974). Investigations using the SS have reported significant multiple correlations between selected factors of the SS and a "robustness" semantic differential measure applied to three concepts: "My Role as a Teacher," "My Principal," and "My Students" (Ellett and Licata 1982). Positive attitudes of elementary teachers on multiple subscales of the SS have also been shown to be significantly and negatively correlated to student perceptions of classroom difficulty, which in turn correlates negatively with achievement (Ellett, Payne, Masters, and Pool 1977).

The Learning Environment Inventory has been extensively used in research studies in England, Australia, Canada, India, and the United States. Perkins (1976), using partial canonical correlation techniques, found that elementary students' perceptions of the school environment significantly related to student achievement and attendance when variance in teacher attitudes was removed from those relations. Using secondary students' perceptions of LEI subscales, significant multiple correlations have been demonstrated between goal direction, cohesiveness, lack of competitiveness, and diversity, and a "robustness" semantic differential applied to the concept "My School" (Licata, Willower, and Ellett 1978). Meta-analyses of studies relating students' perceptions of the social-psychological environments of their classes to learning outcomes have shown positive, significant relationships with many of the LEI subscales (Haertel, Walberg, and Haertel 1979).

Within the ROME validation paradigm, student outcomes were measured by the *Iowa Test of Basic Skills* (ITBS) for grades four and eight and the *Tests of Academic Progress* (TAP) for grade eleven. Attendance figures, computed as a percentage of average daily attendance (ADA) for the twenty-day period most closely approximating the time other data were collected, served as a second measure of student outcome.

Schools' mean scores on the PPDS forms, SS, LEI or MS, ITBS or TAP, and ADA were used as units of analysis in a test of the criterion-related validity of the PPDS with 45 principals in 35 elementary and 10 secondary schools in Georgia. In these schools the various inventories were administered to 3,613 secondary and 3,350 elementary students, 1,200 teachers, and 45 principals (Payne et al. 1975).

Payne and colleagues (1975) summarized the large number of correlations of items, subscales, and student-outcome variables involved in the forty-five school, PPDS validation field test. They calculated the average percentages of significant correlations between items and subscales for elementary schools, secondary schools, and the total sample. The percentage of significant correlations for PPDS item and subscale scores from the various assessment sources and subscales of the SS and MS inventories was 18.1. The figure for secondary schools was 12.1 percent. Combining the data for the elementary and secondary schools, the significant item-subscale correlations increased to 29.2 percent. Significant relationships between assessments of principals' performance and student outcomes (achievement and attendance) were 9.9 percent for the elementary schools, 8.1 percent for the secondary schools, and 23.2 percent for all forty-five schools. The percentage of significant relationships between mediating variables and student-outcome variables was 38.3 for the elementary schools, 13.5 for the secondary schools, and 50.2 for the combined sample.

The results of the PPDS field test conceptually supported the paradigm of the influence of principals' performance on student achievement and attendance as being mediated by teacher and student perceptions of important characteristics of the school environment. The SS was the most predictable criterion measure and was relatively independent of student perceptions of the school environment. Further, the teacher form of the PPDS demonstrated the greatest validity for assessing principals' performances among the various PPDS forms (Payne et al. 1975).

The findings also showed that teachers' positive attitudes about the work environment and higher student achievement are associated with student reports of infrequent interaction with the principal. Student satisfaction with school climate, perception of the easiness of schoolwork, and positive attitudes about a lack of school structure were also related to student reports of infrequent interaction with the principal. Payne and colleagues (1975) and Ellett and Walberg (1979) speculate that a "student independence" factor might require little interaction between students and principals in cases where teacher morale is high and students are learning. These relationships seem to support the notion that the performance of a principal is mediated by its own consequences or other variables, such as teacher and student attitudes, and is indirectly linked to student achievement.

The Project ROME research suggests that the principal is a key element in stimulating staff morale in the school, which, in turn, influences the quality of the classroom climate and the level of subsequent school outcomes. This finding is conceptually consistent with the findings of Block (1983) and the instructional management role of the principal described by Bossert and colleagues (1982).

Challenge Effectiveness and Contingency Theory

The notions that (1) leaders have certain style preferences and (2) particular styles work better in certain types of contexts or situations characterize the nature of contingency theory. Contingency theory describes a leader's style as either relatively relationship-oriented or relatively task-oriented. Favorable situations have good leader-member relations, clear task structure, and a leader with strong power to reward and punish subordinates. Unfavorable situations exhibit poor leader-member relations, vague task structure, and weak power. Through a natural mix of these situational variables, eight types of situations, or octants, emerge on a continuum ranging from favorable to unfavorable. Contingency theory predicts that task-oriented leaders are effective in the most and least favorable situations and that relationship-oriented leaders are more effective in moderately favorable situations.

In an extensive study of managers employed by American Telephone and Telegraph (AT&T) positive relationships were established between managers' perceptions of job challenge and their promotion to higher levels of management. Using assessment center procedures and multiple measures, managers' perceptions of their work being stimulating or challenging accounted for the most variance in the relationship between work situation and managerial promotion or success. Managers assessed as being likely to succeed or unlikely to succeed when given challenging work exhibited a higher success rate than other managers, regardless of prior assessed predictions of promotability or managerial success (Bray, Campbell, and Grant 1974).

These findings seem to suggest that a stimulating or challenging situation motivates managerial effort and that such effort leads to improved performance by the manager and favorable judgments by superiors about the manager's effectiveness and promotability. Once this cycle was set in motion, these managers appeared more likely to be placed in another challenging situation on reassignment, probably as a result of their reputation for success in such circumstances (Bray et al. 1974).

While the AT&T study described managers' performance in a challenging situation in private industry, Peregrine (1982) explored the fruitfulness of contingency theory and the AT&T findings in understanding the effectiveness of school principals. The study involved the principals and faculties of fifty-two elementary schools from two school districts in the central United States. Peregrine hypothesized that principals working in situations that favor their leadership style perceive their role as more challenging than do principals working where their styles do not favor the situation. Consistent with contingency theory, Peregrine predicted that teachers' perceptions of their principal's effectiveness would be significantly higher if the principal works in situations favorable to his or her style than if the principal works in situations that do not favor his or her style. Further, a significant positive correlation was hypothesized between principals' perceptions of job challenge and teachers' perceptions of the principals' effectiveness.

Principals completed three instruments. They responded to the *Least Preferred Coworker* (LPC) scale, a measure of leaders' style preferences. A low LPC score suggests a task-oriented preference and a high LPC score suggests a relationship-oriented preference. The *Task Structure* (TS) scale measures the degree to which school administration tasks are verifiable, clear in their goals, and understood in terms of limited goal paths and specific solutions. The *Robustness Semantic Differential* (RSD) was employed to measure principals' perception of their job challenge. Principals responded to the concept "My Role is . . .," using scales like challenging–dull, fresh–stale, or action-packed–uneventful (Licata and Willower 1978).

Teachers responded to the *Position Power* (PP) scale, an eighteen-item measure of teachers' perceptions of the principal's power to reward and punish. The *Group Atmosphere Scale* (GAS), a ten-item semantic differential measure of leader (principal)-member (teacher) relations, was completed by teachers. They also responded to a shortened, twenty-eight-item version of the *Principal Performance Description Survey* (PPDS) (Ellett and Payne 1978), which uses only the effectiveness scales as a measure of principals' effectiveness.

Based on teachers' mean scores for the GAS, PP, and principals' scores for the TS and LPC, school principals were classified according to contingency theory octants and divided into two groups: (1) schools in which principals' style preference (LPC) and situation (PP, GAS, TS) were favorably matched according to contingency assumptions and (2) schools in which principals' style preference and situation were not matched favorably.

Forty out of the fifty-two principals exhibited a task-oriented management style. Overall, principals tended to view their roles as relatively challenging, and teachers tended to rate principals as relatively effective. In terms of situational variables, principals perceived their roles as having relatively high task structure, and teachers viewed principals as having relatively high position power and positive relations with group members (Peregrine 1982).

No significant relationship between principals' style-situation match and principals' perception of job challenge was established. Additionally, no significant relationship between situational favorableness and principals' perceived job challenge or between style preference and challenge was evident. However, there was a significant, though moderate, relationship ($r = 0.25$) between teachers' PPDS effectiveness scores for staff performance and principals' perception of job challenge.

While a principal's RSD scores or perceived challenge were not significantly related to variables like task structure (TS), position power (PP), and teacher-member relations (GAS), they were significantly associated with the principal's sex, educational background, size of the school, and the school's grade structure. Female principals, principals with less formal education, principals in smaller schools, and principals in schools containing fewer grade levels saw their roles as relatively challenging. Female principals tended to be in smaller schools and had higher GAS and PPDS scores than their male counterparts (Peregrine 1982).

A test of contingency theory, using PPDS mean effectiveness scores as the criterion measure, produced no significant relationships. Principals in situations in which their style preference was favorably matched had only slightly higher but not significantly higher mean PPDS scores than principals in situations not matched to style. However, situational favorableness (higher GAS, TS, PP) was significantly related to teachers' PPDS scores of their principal's effectiveness ($r = 0.54$). This relationship is probably heavily influenced by positive leader-member relations (GAS scores). These were positively correlated ($r = 0.46$) to PPDS effectiveness scores.

Findings from a factor analysis of PPDS data for 566 teachers and from alpha reliability analyses confirmed a four-factor structure with high internal consistency (0.91 to 0.94). These findings, coupled with the PPDS correlations with situational favorableness and teachers' positive sentiments about the school's professional relationships, are consistent with previous PPDS validation results (Payne et al. 1975; Ellett 1976) and support applicability of the PPDS in assessing the effectiveness of the principalship in diverse contexts.

SOME PROPOSITIONS

The purpose of this chapter is to produce some theories, generalizations or propositions, and theoretical insights about principals' effectiveness by triangulating findings from the four research studies summarized. Four tentative propositions about the principalship emerge as a result of this informal triangulation. The propositions are presented to promote future inquiries about the principalship and principals' effective performance.

Effective Principals as Leaders

What are effective principals like as individuals? While the work by Blumberg and Greenfield (1980), qualitative in its approach, provides considerable insight into effective principals, caution about their findings is suggested by their observation that two years after their interviews only one of their out-of-the-ordinary principals was still satisfied with the principalship and interested in continuing. These principals had vision, the need to take charge, the courage to be proactive, and the ability to structure their roles so that they could accomplish their priorities. They also hoped to involve others in decision making and to give and receive good-natured fellowship. Such individuals appear to exhibit characteristics often attributed to leaders in general, even charismatic leaders in other roles and in other contexts. As is often the case with such leaders, and is apparently the case with most of the out-of-the-ordinary principals, these individuals are usually visible, dynamic, but only short-term change agents.

Again, only one of the original eight principals was still satisfied after two years with his job and continued to exhibit the potential to have a long-range impact on his school. At least two explanations are possible. Lipham and Francke (1966) and Licata and Hack (1980) have described principals who are ambitious, innovative, and up-wardly mobile in their careers. They tend to spend little time in teaching, develop sponsors who help them gain visibility with supe-riors, and have aspirations beyond the principalship, which they see as a stepping-stone position. Many of what researchers and others call "effective" principals may fall into this category. One of Peregrine's findings, that principals' perception of job challenge is inversely related to the level of their formal education, might suggest that the more formal education principals accumulate, the more likely they are to see upward mobility as a viable career path and the less likely they are to be challenged by the principalship.

Another explanation for the out-of-the-ordinary principals' even-tual disillusionment might be the friction that occurs when aggressive, proactive leaders interact in a school environment that is not often suited for dramatic changes, particularly in terms of the values and norms of the system. The strength of character exhibited by these principals may provide some protection from the emotional toxicity of the roles. However, this constant friction may, over time, be discouraging. For example, removing an incompetent teacher, as noted by the out-of-the-ordinary principals, can be difficult, frustrating, and costly in maintaining friendly work relations in the school. George McKenna, the principal at George Washington High noted at the beginning of this chapter, replaced 85 percent of the school's teaching staff in an effort to improve his school (Garcia 1983). One can imagine the emotional toll this behavior and its consequences might take on such principals over time.

The characteristics of the sample described by Peregrine (1982) may provide this discussion with another perspective. Recall that in his sample forty of the fifty-two principals indicated a task-oriented style preference (different from Carroll's [1978] report that only 17 percent of his sample had such an orientation). In general, the fifty-two principals tended to view their roles as relatively challenging, and teachers saw them as having relatively positive group-member relations, position power, and effectiveness. This is hardly the description of a beleaguered, "burnt-out" occupational group. These characteristics suggest that relatively effective principals may be widely dispersed in the population of school administrators and not so out of the ordinary. While ambition to move up in administration is probably on the minds of some (probably a healthy sign for the profession), others may opt to stay, learn how to cope with the insecurity and toxicity of the environment, and maintain a reasonable degree of effectiveness in their role. Unlike the principals noted by Blumberg and Greenfield (1980), and more like those described by Wolcott (1973), these principals may be less visible but just as important as others studied.

Given the cautions noted above, descriptions of effective principals seem to have at least one thing in common. *Descriptions of effective principals tend to use words and phrases typically reserved for the characterization of leaders.* This is a conclusion Blumberg and Greenfield (1980) present in their work, which is not surprising. They describe effective principals as resourceful people who like to take charge and work with others to proactively solve problems—effective principals are persons of vision. Further, leaders are often considered innovative. The finding by Miskel (1977) that innovation effort is positively related to other measures of principals' effectiveness suggests that effective principals, as might be expected, sometimes show leadership in bringing about positive changes in their schools. Whether such descriptions are applied to individuals who adapt well or poorly or to individuals who stay briefly or for an entire career, the following proposition might be advanced to reflect the theme of principals as leaders:

P_1: The performances and qualities that are used to describe effective principals are also employed to characterize leadership or leaders in various contexts and roles.

Caplow (1976) has summarized the characteristics associated with leaders in various organizations and claims that the leaders are typically very intelligent, exhibit high energy or effort levels, and show concern for their followers; but when they are given a choice between organizational goals and their followers' desires, leaders will invariably choose organizational goals. These characteristics, coupled with the perception by others that the individual is successful, are alleged to be associated with positive leadership in organizations. While these characteristics are not unlike those attributed to effective principals, the suggestion that leaders are individuals who have organizational success at least in part attributed to them by followers leads us to the next proposition about principals' job challenge.

Job Challenge

What about their job challenges principals? Apparently, when others view them as being effective in their role, principals see their role as challenging. The effectiveness of staff personnel seems to be important in this relationship. This is not surprising in light of findings by Miskel (1977), Payne and colleagues (1975), Ellett (1976), and Peregrine (1982), which note significant positive relationships between teachers' perceptions of the quality of their work environment and principals' effectiveness. Findings from these more recent research studies are conceptually consistent with earlier examinations of principals' leadership (Gross and Herriott 1965).

Ellett and Walberg (1979) have posited that much of a principal's perception, intention, and subsequent behavior can be understood by evaluating the consequences of his or her previous behavior. This insight may suggest that when a principal's performance is positively evaluated by others in the school (positive consequence of certain behavior), the principal's perception of these positive evaluations can be in part understood as a feeling of challenge or "arousal"—a desire to continue with enthusiasm! Challenge appears to be stimulated by others' perception of principals' effectiveness, not by situational favorableness or adversity, a particular style preference of the principal, or a match between style and situation. Thus, we put forth the next proposition:

P_2: Principals are challenged or aroused by the perception that others (particularly teachers) see them as performing effectively.

Compared to their male counterparts, female elementary principals, particularly those in smaller, less complex elementary schools, tended to have more positive group-member relations, higher PPDS effectiveness scores, and subsequently viewed their role as more challenging (Peregrine 1982). Even though the other three studies examined in this chapter found no comparable set of findings, it is important to note that differences between the performance of male and female principals have been described more than once in the literature. Meskin (1978) presents a recent summary of these findings that suggest that compared to male principals, female elementary principals have higher performance ratings, more-capable students, more concern for individualized instruction, better supervision of instruction, and more-professional teachers. Gross and Trask (1964) noted that female principals typically spend more years in teaching than males and that this may explain why females are more committed and confident in directing instructional progress. Keeping these findings in mind, a third proposition might be advanced:

P_3: Female elementary principals tend to be more effective and more challenged by their role in school organizations than are their male counterparts.

Effectiveness and the School Environment

Miskel's (1977) findings suggest that teachers' positive perceptions of their school's interpersonal climate are associated with positive effectiveness ratings of the principal's performance. Ellett and Walberg (1979) note that comprehensive measures of the performance of principals have been shown to significantly and positively relate to teachers' perceptions of the quality of their work environment and to students' perceptions of the school climate, and that these views of the school environment are positively related to student achievement and attendance. Peregrine (1982) reports a positive relationship between situational favorableness, particularly teachers' positive perceptions of leader-members relations and ratings of principals' effectiveness. These findings seem to suggest a generalization summarized in the following proposition:

P_4: There is a positive reciprocal association between principals' effectiveness and teachers' perceptions of the quality of their work environment and school outcomes.

This proposition seems congruent with notions in the field, and to a degree in the research community, that principals set or maintain the environment in which effective teaching and learning take place and, at the same time, are influenced by the school environment and outcomes. Apparently, a school principal's performance influences the positive or negative sentiments of others about school operation and the quality of the school work environment. These sentiments, in turn, are more directly linked to important school outcomes such as student achievement. We have characterized these relationships as being reciprocal in order to emphasize the multiple causal patterns and directions between and among these variables.

TOWARD A MODEL OF PERFORMANCE EVALUATION AND ORGANIZATIONAL EFFECTIVENESS

In a paper on leadership and educational administration, Bridges (1979) noted that the literature often used in training aspiring school administrators regularly portrays proper performance in administration as heroic and proactive, which suggests indirectly that administrators are often the most important "independent" variable in schooling. He notes that leadership is usually described in lofty terms and that the difficulties of the role are generally marked by discussion of the pleasurable and stimulating possibilities of effective performance. Bias suggesting that the administrator is the chief initiator of action and determiner of consequences has possibly been part of both complex and simplistic treatments of administration. This independent variable—bias—seems to persist in spite of research findings and commonsense observations suggesting that leaders are not always masters of their own destinies or the destiny of schools as organizations. (See Lowin and Craig 1968 as an example.)

For example, among the four studies reviewed in this paper, Blumberg and Greenfield (1980) present situational frustrations that their principals felt powerless to control; Miskel (1977) noted that school innovation effort is more significantly associated with the level of school-district technology than with the effectiveness of principals; and Ellett and Walberg (1979) emphasize an interactive view of the effectiveness of the principals over more simplistic one-way, causal models. Given these findings and the propositions advanced above, it would seem fruitful to continue our examination of the effectiveness of principals not in terms of the simplistic independent variable of bias that Bridges warns against, but more in terms of an interactive view like that presented by Ellett and Walberg (1979).

Every school social system is composed of individuals and roles. Individuals take the roles of principal, teacher, student, parent, central-office administrator, or community member, just to name a few. Performance in a particular organizational role can be understood by looking at the formal organization's role expectations, the individual's attempt to adapt to the norms and values of the informal organization, and efforts by each individual to meet his or her own needs (Getzels and Guba 1957).

Each role performance by a principal, for instance, is evaluated by the principal and potentially every other individual in the system. Based on the principal's analysis of this behavior and on the consequences and evaluations of the behavior by self and others, the principal has the opportunity to decide whether previous behavior is consistent with the role expectations, norms, and values of the organization and with his or her personal needs. This performance-evaluation cycle may be true for every person and role in the school setting.

While it may well be the case that leadership from the principal, because of its symbolic and superordinate-subordinate authority, has the potential to initiate substantial change in schools, it is difficult to conceive of such behavior being successful without positive evaluation by others in the larger social system. For instance, principals like Adan Salgado in Austin, Texas, or Frances Vazquez in the Bronx, New York, wished to turn their schools around, but were able to do so only by "mobilizing" students, teachers, parents, and the central office toward that end. While in these cases the principal was apparently the initiator of change, in other schools changes could be caused by community pressure, pressure from teachers, students, central office, even the government. Once change begins, the historical cause or initial independent variable is difficult to identify in a complex interplay of behaviors, evaluations, and subsequent behaviors. While this framework does not discount the generalizations of propositions one through four, it instead suggests that these relationships may well exist but should be understood as only parts of a larger interactive social setting.

Further, it may be possible to take this framework and apply it more directly in describing effectiveness and positive sentiments about organizations, which is often termed "morale." For instance, it might be posited that each evaluation of the performance of self and others carries with it a hypothetical positive, negative, or neutral value and that the summation of these values for the individual and the formal organization is understood as *effectiveness*, and for individuals and the informal organization it is understood as *morale*. In other words, and as an example, the effectiveness of a formal role such as the principalship or of the entire school organization can be understood by reviewing the various evaluations made of formal role expectations and organizational goals. Morale, on the other hand, might be understood as informal organization evaluations of performances according to whether or not these behaviors are congruent with individual needs, group norms, and values of the informal system. For instance, one might speculate that teachers positively evaluate principals' performances that show respect for teachers' discretionary power in the classroom. This is consistent with the needs, norms, and values of the teacher subculture and with expectations of the principal's role as an instructional supervisor. Such evaluations are probably pertinent both to principals' effectiveness as perceived by superordinates and to teachers' (subordinates') morale.

Since evaluations in the formal or informal system may overlap or interact, this may explain why teachers' judgments of principals' effectiveness are often associated with teachers' positive sentiments about their work environment. Using this perspective, interactive explanations may be more meaningful than simple causal descriptions. Further, it would seem that the potential for change in such systems increases with the number and diversity of possible evaluations and evaluation sources.

Taking this conceptualization further, it might be hypothesized that individuals and organizations tend to adapt and adjust their behavior to the requirements of performance evaluations in order to meet their own needs. This notion, suggested also in part by Thompson (1967), explains behavior as being adaptive but also dependent on the needs of individuals involved in the situation. For instance, George McKenna, principal of George Washington High, could have just gone along with the deplorable conditions he faced when he arrived on the job, but that apparently would be out of character for this former civil rights activist. His individual needs greatly affected how he adapted and adjusted to his new job. Obviously, if he had had a different set of needs, things may not have worked out so well. Further, others in the school setting must have agreed with McKenna's evaluations of the situation and supported his performance.

Even though a school could become unintentionally dysfunctional for students, and new members could be vulnerable to the evaluations and pressures from the school's veteran members to conform, change is always possible. For example, an ambitious, upwardly mobile principal, teachers who are just "fed up," or a parent with some strange ideas about school might try to disconfirm a significant number of performance evaluations within the system in order to bring about change. Whatever the source, subsequent changes or improved effectiveness and morale apparently are almost always understood as an interactive process of performances, evaluations, and subsequent performances of many actors. Schools are complex social organizations, and the roles and behaviors of effective school principals are multidimensional.

CONCLUSION

In this chapter we reviewed four studies on principals' effectiveness that employ somewhat diverse methodological and theoretical frameworks. This was done in order to triangulate the findings and identify some themes, directions, and insights. Four generalizations were derived from cross-checking findings from some or all of the studies. These generalizations suggest that effective principals tend to be described in terms often employed to characterize leaders rather than administrators or managers. Principals tend to be challenged or stimulated by the perceptions of others, particularly teachers, that they are performing effectively. Teachers perceive female elementary principals as being more effective and having better leader-member relations than male principals. As individuals, females see their job as more challenging than do their male counterparts. Teachers' scores of principals' effectiveness are positively related to teachers' sentiments about the quality of their work environment.

Consistent with notions described by Ellett and Walberg (1979), the studies reviewed suggest that each performance by an individual in the school context is evaluated by self and others. These evaluations interact with one another and often result in modification of subsequent performance. The summation of evaluations of performance against formal role expectations can be considered *effectiveness*. Evaluations of performance according to the norms and values of the informal system can be considered *morale*. Individuals and organizations tend to adapt and adjust to these evaluations in order to meet their own goals or needs. Thus, change can be understood by this adaptation process, or individuals' attempts to meet their needs as well as the adaptive requirements of the school as a social system.

Echoing Bridges (1979) and Ellett and Walberg (1979), we argue in this chapter for interactive explanations of the principalship rather than simple one-way causal paths. The principal is viewed not as *the* initiator of change or determiner of organizational consequences, but as *an* important interactor in bringing about positive outcomes. Thus, effective peformance may best be defined by the behavioral consequences and the "systemic" evaluations (Licata 1983) that help shape such behavior and that reflect the particular needs and characteristics of the individual principal.

REFERENCES

Anderson, Gary J. *The Assessment of Learning Environments: A Manual for the Learning Environment Inventory.* Halifax, Nova Scotia: Atlantic Institute of Education, 1973.

Baumgartel, Howard, and Jeanpierre, Francoise, "Applying New Knowledge in Back Home Settings: A Study of Indian Managers' Adaptive Efforts." *Journal of Applied Behavioral Science* 7, no. 6 (1972): 674–694.

Block, Allen W., ed. *Effective Schools: A Summary of Research.* Arlington, Va.: Educational Research Service, 1983.

Blumberg, Arthur, and Greenfield, William. *The Effective Principal: Perspectives on School Leadership.* Boston: Allyn and Bacon, 1980.

Bossert, Stephen T.; Dwyer, David C.; Rowan, Brian; and Lee, Ginny V. "The Instructional Management Role of the Principal." *Educational Administration Quarterly* 18 (Summer 1982): 34–64.

Bray, Douglas W.; Campbell, Richard J.; and Grant, Donald L. *Formative Years in Business.* New York: Krieger, 1974.

Bridges, Edwin M. "The Nature of Leadership." Paper prepared for the conference on Educational Administration Twenty Years Later: 1954–1974. Columbus: Ohio State University, 1979.

Caplow, Theodore. *Principles of Organization.* New York: McGraw-Hill, 1966.

Caplow, Theodore. *How to Run Any Organization.* Hinsdale, Ill.: Dryden Press, 1976.

Carroll, Patricia A. "Central Life Interests and Sources of Attachment to Work among School Administrators." Ph.D. dissertation, Syracuse University, 1978.

Coughlan, Robert J. "Dimensions of Teacher Morale." *American Educational Research Journal* 7 (March 1970): 221–235.

Coughlan, Robert J., and Cooke, Robert A. "Work Attitudes." In *Evaluating Educational Performance*, edited by Herbert J. Walberg. Berkeley, Calif.: McCutchan Publishing Corp., 1974.

Denzin, Norman K. *The Research Act.* Chicago: Aldine Publishing Co., 1970.

Ellett, Chad D. "The Continued Refinement and Development of the Georgia Principal Assessment System and Its Application to a Field-based Training Program for Public School Principals: Assessment Design, Procedures, Instrumentation, Field Test Results." Project Report, vol. 1. Athens: Georgia Department of Education and the College of Education, University of Georgia, 1976.

Ellett, Chad D., and Licata, Joseph W. "Teacher Perceptions of Organizational Roles, Robustness, and Work Environment." *Journal of Educational Administration* 10, no. 1 (1982): 33–44.

Ellett, Chad D., and Payne, David A. *Principal Performance Description Survey: User's Guide.* Athens: Georgia Department of Education and the College of Education, University of Georgia, 1978.

Ellett, Chad D.; Payne, David A.; Masters, John A.; and Pool, Jonelle. "The Relationship between Teacher and Student Perceptions of School Environment Dimensions and School Outcome Variables." Paper presented at the Annual Meeting of the Southeastern Psychological Association, Miami, Fla., 1977.

Ellett, Chad D., and Walberg, Herbert J. "Principals' Competency, Environment, and Outcomes." In *Improving Educational Standards and Productivity: The Research Basis for Policy*, edited by Herbert J. Walberg. Berkeley, Calif.: McCutchan Publishing Corp., 1979.

Garcia, Guy D. "Hope Stirs in the Ghetto." *Time*, 25 April 1983.

Getzels, Jacob A., and Guba, Egon G. "Social Behavior and the Administrative Process." *School Review* 65 (December 1957): 423–441.

Gross, Neal, and Herriott, Robert E. *Staff Leadership in Public Schools: A Sociological Inquiry*. New York: Wiley, 1965.

Gross, Neal, and Trask, Anne E. *Men and Women as Elementary Principals*. Final Report No. 2, Cooperative Research Project No. 853. Cambridge, Mass.: Graduate School of Education, Harvard University, 1964.

Haertel, Geneva D.; Walberg, Herbert J.; and Haertel, Edward. "Social-Psychological Environments and Learning: A Quantitative Synthesis." Paper presented at the Annual Meeting of the American Educational Research Association, San Francisco, 1979.

Laing, Ronald. *The Divided Self*. New York: Pantheon Books, 1969.

Levinson, Harry. *The Great Jackass Fallacy*. Boston: Division of Research, Graduate Studies of Business Administration, Harvard University, 1973.

Levinson, Harry. *Organizational Diagnosis*. Cambridge, Mass.: Harvard University Press, 1973.

Lewin, Kurt. *Field Theory and Social Service*. New York: Harper and Row, 1951.

Licata, Joseph W. "Systemic Appraisal of Educational Leadership Personnel." In *Evaluating Administrative Performance: Current Trends and Techniques*, edited by Elio Zapulla, pp. 281–303. Belmont, Calif.: Star Publishing Co., 1983.

Licata, Joseph W., and Hack, Walter G. "School Administrator Grapevine Structure." Educational Administration Quarterly 16 (Fall 1980): 82–99.

Licata, Joseph W., and Willower, Donald J. "Toward an Operational Definition of Environmental Robustness." *Journal of Educational Research* 71, no. 4 (1978): 219–222.

Licata, Joseph W.; Willower, Donald J.; and Ellett, Chad D. "School and Environmental Robustness." *Journal of Experimental Education* 47 (Fall 1978): 28–34.

Lipham, James, and Francke, Donald C. "Nonverbal Behavior of Administrators." *Educational Administration Quarterly* 2 (Spring 1966): 101–109.

Lowin, Aaron, and Craig, James R. "The Influence of Level of Performance on Managerial Style: An Experimental Object-Lesson in the Ambiguity of Correlational Data." *Organizational Behavior and Human Performance* 3 (November 1968): 440–458.

Meskin, Joan D. "Women as Principals." In *The Principal in Metropolitan Schools*, edited by Donald A. Erickson and Theodore L. Reller. Berkeley, Calif.: McCutchan Publishing Corp., 1978.

Miskel, Cecil G. "Principals' Perceived Effectiveness, Innovation Effort, and the School Situation." *Educational Administration Quarterly* 13, no. 1 (1977): 31–46.

Payne, David A.; Ellett, Chad D.; Perkins, Mark L.; Klein, Alice E.; and Shellinberger, Sylvia. *The Verification and Validation of Principal Competencies and Performance Indicators: Assessment Design, Procedures, Instrumentation. Field Test Results*. Final Project Report, vol. 1. Athens: Georgia Department of Education and College of Education, University of Georgia, 1975.

Peregrine, Phillip E. "The Robustness of Managerial Life in Schools: A Test of Contingency Theory." Ph.D. dissertation, Ohio State University, 1982.

Perkins, Mark L. "Canonical Correlational Analysis of the Relationship among School Climate, Teacher Morale, and the Educationally Relevant Performance of Fourth Grade Students." Ph.D. dissertation, University of Georgia, 1976.

Thompson, James D. *Organizations in Action.* New York: McGraw-Hill, 1967.

Walberg, Herbert J. "A Theory of Educational Productivity." Paper presented at the Annual Meeting of the Georgia Educational Research Association, Atlanta, 1978.

Williamson, John B.; Karp, David A.; and Dalphin, John R. *The Research Craft.* Boston: Little, Brown, 1977.

Wofford, Jerry C. "Managerial Behavior, Situational Factors, Productivity and Morale." *Administrative Science Quarterly* 16 (March 1971): 10–18.

Wolcott, Harry F. *The Man in the Principal's Office.* New York: Holt, Rinehart and Winston, 1973.

9

School Success and the Organizational Conditions of Teaching

Susan J. Rosenholtz

Until recently, studies of inner-city elementary schools serving low-SES, minority students had painted quite a dismal and discouraging picture. Research during the last decade, however, has produced some anomalous findings—rare instances where inner-city schools have produced standardized achievement test results for low-SES youngsters that far exceed those of schools serving identical populations. The success of these effective schools, I will argue, resides primarily in the organizational conditions of teaching. I will show that organizational factors influence teacher behavior by influencing the degree of teacher commitment and the degree to which norms and values are shared among teachers and administrators.

TEACHER COMMITMENT

My analysis pivots fundamentally upon an assumption about teacher commitment. Central to a school's success is its ability to motivate teachers to make continual contributions to it rather than to some competing organization or endeavor. Teacher commitment and

An expanded version of this chapter appeared in the *American Journal of Education* 93 (1985): 352–387. Reprinted with permission from the University of Chicago Press.

its attendant behaviors, however, are not categorical or unvarying commodities. They depend to no small extent on the incentives and opportunities offered by the school and on the organizational conditions under which teachers work. In particular, teachers are motivated to remain in a setting and productively contribute only if the inducements offered them are at least as great as the contributions they are asked to make (March and Simon 1958). In other words, the rewards of teaching must outweigh the frustrations.

The primary rewards for most teachers come from students' academic accomplishments—from feeling certain about their own capacity to affect student development (Bishop 1977; Bredeson, Fruth, and Kasten 1983; Glenn and McLean 1981; Lortie 1975; McLaughlin and Marsh 1978). Indeed, teacher certainty about professional practice highly correlates with student achievement (Ashton, Webb, and Doda 1983; Armor et al. 1976; Azumi and Madhere 1983; Brookover et al. 1979).

Relatively speaking, the proportion of psychic rewards accruing to teachers in most urban settings is often lower than that in other settings. Low-SES students seem to have more difficulty making academic progress; they are seen as being more aggressive and less respectful and as having a negative attitude toward learning (Azumi and Madhere 1983; Levy 1970; Leacock 1969; Warren 1975). Because of these conditions, most inner-city schoolteachers complain that their custodial function far outweighs their educative function (Leacock 1969; Levy 1970; Warren 1975). This takes on additional significance in light of findings that the number of behavioral sanctions teachers administer during classroom instructional time correlates negatively with student achievement (Fisher et al. 1980; Good and Grouws 1977; Stallings 1980). Thus, just as student learning is the primary source of psychic rewards for teachers, difficult relations with students is the primary source of psychic debilitation (Bredeson et al. 1983; Coates and Thoresen 1978). Although the absence of student disruption does not automatically imply teachers' acquisition of psychic rewards, it is a necessary condition along the way.

A striking exception to the above is the instructionally effective urban school. Relative to most inner-city schools, in effective schools the rewards earned through work with students are far greater. Plihal (1982) found, in fact, that successful inner-city teachers place greater emphasis and importance on the rewards resulting from student learning than do successful teachers in the suburbs. It may well be that success with inner-city students is a particularly satisfying career accomplishment. This interpretation is supported by Lortie's (1975) interviews of teachers. In response to questions about craft pride, teachers placed special emphasis on success with students whom others considered to be beyond help. It is therefore not surprising that teachers in successful inner-city schools report feeling greater certainty about the technology of teaching than do teachers serving low-SES students in less successful schools (Ashton, Webb, and Doda 1983; Armor et al. 1976; Azumi and Madhere 1983; Glenn and McLean 1981).

The fact that the rewards of teaching vary with school-level factors underscores the strength of organizational inducements in mobilizing the commitment and involvement of teachers. In this chapter I explore organizational conditions that provide teachers with the needed inducement to make contributions to inner-city schools. I will point to the importance of goals as a means of both ascertaining school effectiveness and motivating and directing organizational activities within the school. The effective school, I will argue, relies almost exclusively on its organizational goals as the incentive to attract and motivate teachers. Teachers enlist because they want to assist in helping to achieve the goals espoused by the school, and the school, in achieving its goals, provides sufficient inducements to teachers to secure a continuing flow of contributions.

THE IMPORTANCE OF GOALS

I make a second assumption about factors explaining the success of effective schools. Compared to their less effective counterparts, effective schools have tighter congruence between the values, norms, and behaviors of principals and teachers, and the managerial-level activities align closely with and facilitate those of the technical level. In short, because there is consensus on school goals, principals and teachers act in unison to achieve them.

The importance of shared values and goals should not be underestimated. Agreement about school goals and the means to achieve them increases the school's capacity for rational planning and action.

There is an organizational basis for directing behavior, for motivating behavior, for justifying behavior, and for evaluating behavior. In the next section I address precisely how this consensus on school life develops and its implications for the subsequent behavior of principals and teachers.

THE BEHAVIOR OF PRINCIPALS AND STAFF MOBILIZATION

Principals' Attitudes and Behavior

Uncertainty about the technology of teaching and its capacity to bring about positive changes in student achievement is the enemy of rational planning and action. Ineffective principals, uncertain that changes in student performance can actually be brought about, appear not to act in ways that make student learning possible. When students fail to make academic progress in unsuccessful schools, principals vilify teachers and students as the culprits (see, for example, Brookover et al. 1979; CSDE 1980; Levy 1970; Morris 1982). From the ineffective principal's viewpoint, it may make no sense to set academic goals if teachers or students seem incapable of reaching them.

In contrast, effective principals convey certainty that teachers can improve student performance and that students themselves are capable of learning. Goals of high student achievement are almost always at the forefront of effective principals' planning and action. They set explicit operational goals for students' academic performance, and they clearly communicate these goals to their staff members (Coulson 1977; Glenn and McLean 1981; Phi Delta Kappa 1980; Sizemore, Brossard, and Harrigan 1983; Spartz et al. 1977; Weber 1971). For instance, in the elementary schools studied by Venezky and Winfield (1979), successful principals insisted that 60 percent of their student population read at grade level or above. In identifying problems of academic progress, effective principals press for greater commitment from teachers (Armor et al. 1976; Brookover et al. 1979; Rutter et al. 1979; Sizemore, Brossard, and Harrigan 1983) and hold teachers accountable for their actions (CSDE 1980; Glenn and McLean 1981; Hunter 1979; Sizemore, Brossard, and Harrigan 1983; Venezky and

Winfield 1979; Weber 1971; Wellisch et al. 1978). They refuse to set aside basic skill acquisition even for the lowest achievers (Brookover et al. 1979; Sizemore, Brossard, and Harrigan 1983; Wellisch et al. 1978; Wynne 1980) and insist that students be retained until they meet academic standards (Sizemore, Brossard, and Harrigan 1983; Wellisch et al. 1978; Wynne 1980).

Through these and other actions I describe in the following pages, administrative leaders communicate a certainty that student achievement is linked strongly to teacher effort. Certainty defines and organizes principals' actions to facilitate teachers' effort. In fact, as the reader will learn next, effective principals seek ways to reduce uncertainty so as to increase their capacity for rational planning (Scott 1981). If basic skill acquisition is the operational goal, and teacher effort is the means to attain it, it makes sense to find ways to optimize teacher effort in order to maximize student mastery.

Recruitment and Selection of Teachers

One way to both reduce principals' uncertainty and increase goal consensus among the faculty is to recruit like-minded staff. Not unexpectedly, effective principals recruit and attract teachers who accept and share the prevailing standards and values of the faculty, with the goals of the school serving as focal points around which decisions are made. Wynne (1980), for example, found that although there was nothing obvious about the way hiring decisions were made in ineffective schools, effective school administrators screened applicants carefully, checking references and using interviews to articulate school goals and expectations. In a finding similar to Wynne's, the principals of eight effective inner-city schools described in the Phi Delta Kappa study (1980) reported handpicking most members of their staff. Applying schools goals to the selection of teachers appears to serve as an important control for ensuring the school's quality.

While social-class differences between schools bear directly on the school's ability to attract teachers (Lortie 1973), the high visibility of effective schools increases the probability that they will be distinguished from others, thereby enhancing their chances for success in recruitment. Indeed, in Spuck's (1974) study, schools demonstrating high levels of pride in meeting goals and positive interaction among faculty accounted for 43 percent of the variance in ease of teacher recruitment. Not surprisingly, both of these intrinsic rewards characterize effective inner-city schools. Significantly, the ability to attract and motivate staff, to control the flow of teachers, sustains the homogeneity of values seemingly central to a school's effectiveness.

The importance of careful selection procedures cannot be overemphasized. If principals fail in their efforts to attract good teachers and keep them, they become trapped in a cycle of high turnover and low school productivity. Schools that consistently have large contingents of new recruits are particularly demanding on principals' time because principals are expected to supervise closely the work of inexperienced teachers (Dreeben 1970). In part because they are constrained by high staff turnover and lack of goal consensus, ineffective principals often have less time to devote to the instructional goals of the school. The other side of the coin is that more-effective principals spend less time dealing with the above problems, and thus have more time to move the school toward instructional goals. In essence, effective principals have more time to be effective. In this way, inequalities in educational productivity between schools are maintained.

Teacher Fit

Attracting and selecting outstanding teachers is one problem; having them "fit" is still another. A teacher's effectiveness is not an objective, uniform, or unvarying judgment. It depends heavily on the specific situation into which the teacher is placed, the expectations and behavior of one's colleagues, and the "fit" between the teacher's own behavior and school norms. The same individual who fits poorly into one situation (and is judged to be unsuccessful in it) may fit superbly and successfully into another. Further, although it is easier for new recruits to settle into effective than ineffective schools, occasional problems of fit are bound to arise. Then, too, any principal taking over a new assignment must deal with the unassessed teachers who have been working in the school.

In effective schools teachers who do not fit or who threaten to undermine existing consensual norms meet with strong organizational resistance. They may be isolated from their professional group (Levy 1970; Phi Delta Kappa 1980; Wynne 1980); they may suffer a reduction in resource allocation (Warren 1975; Armor et al. 1976); or, in extreme cases, they may be targeted for removal from the organization (Sizemore, Brossard, and Harrigan 1983; Phi Delta Kappa 1980; Wynne 1980). For instance, Levy (1970) describes the manner in which one effective inner-city principal harrassed and badgered errant teachers who "weren't putting out" until they either modified their behavior or departed. Therefore, it seems that the homogeneity of values among staff in effective schools is protected from disturbance in two important ways: by carefully controlling the flow of teachers into the school and then by closely monitoring them thereafter.

Induction into Teaching

A second way in which consensus on school purpose develops lies in how teachers are socialized to school norms. Although entrants may come with a propensity to accept school goals, their ultimate adoption of them is in no small way determined by how successfully they are socialized. "Organizational socialization" means the process by which entrants acquire the perspectives and norms of members within the organization. The success of organizational socialization can be observed when individuals take on institutional realities as their own subjective perceptions of what is real. Institutional views become accepted as objective fact rather than as opinion through recurrent patterns of daily interaction; we come to know what is a fact through an interactive process in which each of us learns what others seem to regard as fact. This perspective leads to several propositions about the mark of successful socialization for entering teachers.

Peer Socialization and Collegial Norms

Students of educational sociology distinguish between two normative school settings that give rise to differing patterns of exchange that shape the entrant's notions about the "reality" of the central purpose of teaching within the school and the "reality" of precisely what constitutes good collegial relations (Bishop 1977; Little 1982; Lortie 1975).

One setting is characterized by isolation from professional knowledge. Isolation in schools results from a cellular division in which teachers spend large portions of their days separated physically from colleagues, without the benefit of seeing or hearing them. In isolated settings, teachers believe they alone are responsible for running their classrooms and that to do so successfully requires a maximum amount of autonomy. Requests for assistance among staff members frequently are interpreted as a lack of teaching competence (Bishop 1977; Lortie 1975). For example, Glidewell and colleagues (1983), sampling teachers from ten Chicago elementary schools, found that help-seeking behavior implied a reduction in status among the faculty, and help-giving behavior implied an increase in status among faculty. In fact, teachers considered autonomy to be something of a moral imperative; they felt clear moral constraint against offering suggestions to other teachers about even the most routine matters.

Where teachers are cut off from their colleagues for major portions of the day, the effects are profound. First, there is little opportunity to develop collectively held notions about what is important to emphasize in teaching and about how success should be gauged. Indeed, under isolated working conditions, teachers' classroom goals are strikingly individualistic and require indicators of effectiveness based upon individual beliefs about what should be learned (Bishop 1977; Lortie 1975; Tye and Tye 1984).

A second effect of teacher isolation is that informal relations among teachers are unlikely to center around the substance of teaching as a common work activity. When teachers in isolated settings talk together, the substance of their conversations rarely includes instructional topics so that they can avoid making any conclusions about the relative competence implied by requesting or offering assistance. Bishop (1977) found that despite a relatively extensive set of informal networks existing in isolated settings, teachers do not tend to become involved with their friends in work-related issues.

Although Glidewell and colleagues (1983) did find evidence of "experience swapping" in isolated settings where related classroom experiences were somewhat sympathetically shared, Willower and Jones (1963) found that the content of such "swapping" in inner-city elementary schools focused on how teachers handled student discipline problems, demeaning remarks about students' lack of academic success, and aggressive references to hopelessly uncooperative students. Swapping "war stories" among teachers is also noted in Levy's (1970) study of a low-SES school, but teacher conversations there centered also on daily poker games, politics, sports, and the latest trends in clothing and movies.

The significance of such nonproductive exchanges may be that they reinforce disengaged teacher behavior and legitimize ineffective—if not outright deleterious—work with students. That is, non-task-related interactions may provide teachers with a basis for social support and recognition for acts of nonteaching. This occurrence is described by organizational theorists as goal displacement: professional respect is earned not through instructional effectiveness but through the effective use of force (Levy 1970; Willower and Jones 1963). Hence, at its most potent level, isolation plays a major role in creating a disjuncture between a school's professed and operational goals, a disjuncture that becomes readily apparent in ineffective urban schools whose professed aim may be to teach effectively but whose day-to-day activity reveals a different goal, that is, student control.

Effective urban schools are far less likely to be isolated work settings for teachers. Instead, they are usually places of intellectual sharing, collaborative planning, and collegial work. Staff interaction is characterized as task focused, cooperative, and frequent (Armor et al. 1976; CSDE 1980; Phi Delta Kappa 1980; Rutter et al. 1979; Sizemore, Brossard, and Harrigan 1983; Venezky and Winfield 1979; Wynne 1980). Little's (1982) ethnographic study of desegregated elementary schools provides a particularly cogent example. Successful schools were distinguished from less successful schools by patterned norms of collegiality among staff. Underlying collaborative norms is the belief that teaching is a collective rather than an individual undertaking. When compared to teachers in less successful schools, teachers in effective schools interacted to a greater extent on the basis of professional concerns rather than of social chatter and did so with greater frequency and with a greater number of colleagues. Interaction opportunities occurred in training sessions, faculty meetings, teachers' lounges, hallways, and classrooms. Teachers focused efforts to improve on specific teaching practices rather than on particular individuals' behavior.

Bishop's (1977) twenty-four-school study of elementary teachers' informal relations also helps clarify the pivotal position that colleagues occupy in the acquisition of norms and values. Comparing reciprocal associations in isolated and collaborative school settings, Bishop found that the majority of informal associations in isolated settings were primarily friendship-based, whereas in collaborative schools they were both friendship- and instruction-based. In isolated settings teachers did not involve their friends in work-related discussion, but under collaborative conditions friendship and work tended to overlap. As in the Little study, collaborative schools showed more-extensive patterns of mutual association than did isolated schools, indicating greater faculty cohesiveness.

The idea that schools stressing norms of collegiality have more-constructive patterns of faculty interaction is supported by two additional studies. Glidewell and colleagues (1983) found that the frequency of teachers' requests for and offers of assistance was related inversely to experience swapping, and that in schools stressing collaborative norms there was far more mutual problem solving. Further, in Bridges and Hallinan's (1978) sample of teachers within fifty-seven California elementary schools, the extent of collaboration explained more than half the variance in work-relevant communication.

As might be expected, frequent task-focused interaction plays a significant role in the development of school goals. If reality is constructed socially through recurrent patterns of interaction, it follows that greater consensus on school goals emerges from increased task-related interaction among staff (see also March and Simon 1958). It has been seen that the isolated teaching conditions that characterize less successful schools constrain constructive communication, whereas the collaborative arrangements of effective schools enhance it. Frequent conversation about instructional practices and how to improve them, then, increases the likelihood that student achievement will be viewed as a highly salient aspect of school life.

Further, as noted above, greater task-related interaction leads to greater faculty cohesiveness (see, for example, Bridges and Hallinan 1978). The importance of cohesiveness to goal consensus, it seems, is its implied power of collective perception. Cohesiveness among staff members acts to tighten the system of feedback to individuals and presses them to internalize values and goals. That is, as different sources of feedback within the school move toward congruence, the power of peers' collective perceptions produces compelling reasons to internalize that reality. Drawing similar conclusions, Wynne (1980) found reluctance to accept group goals revealed through interaction among staff members. In these conversations, malefactors were subject to powerful sanctions of group disapproval, which ultimately forced either compliance or departure. Thus, the individual's acceptance of group goals is in large measure determined by the strength of group cohesiveness. High group cohesiveness in effective schools directs teachers toward adopting student achievement as their primary mission.

A final noteworthy point is that teachers' adoption of norms and goals occurs over time. The longer individuals work within a school, the greater their potential for interaction, and hence the more consensual their reality of school life. Charters's (1969) study of several St. Louis high schools illustrates well the relationship between interaction patterns and staff stability. Where schools had high continuity of personnel from the end of one academic year to the beginning of the next, virtually no changes in communication patterns occurred. However, where schools experienced high faculty turnover from spring to fall, massive disruption of staff interaction occurred, both in the saturation and frequency of contacts. Staff stability, then, is a necessary condition for continual collegial exchange and, therefore, for the development of consensus about school life.

Norms of collegiality do not simply happen. They do not spring spontaneously out of teachers' respect and concern for one another. Rather, they are carefully engineered by structuring the workplace with frequent exposure to contact and frequent opportunities for interaction. It is clearly a "try it; you'll like it" proposition. Such social engineering in successful schools is the most likely product of the direct intervention of principals. At some schools, time is set aside by principals for faculty meetings during which joint planning and problem solving occur (Coulson 1977; CSDE 1980; Glenn and McLean 1981; Phi Delta Kappa 1980; Sizemore, Brossard, and Harrigan, 1983; Wilson and Corbett 1983). At other schools, principals build opportunities for interaction into in-service programs (Armor et al. 1976; Hunter 1979; Phi Delta Kappa 1980), or formally establish subgroups of faculty who are charged with particular technical responsibilities (Sizemore, Brossard, and Harrigan 1983; Wilson and Corbett 1983; Wynne 1980).

That communication patterns among staff members of effective schools initially depend upon directives from principals is clearly demonstrated in Charters's (1969) study. Following high spring turnover in the faculty of one exemplary high school, communication patterns the following fall became centralized around an administrative cadre who served as connecting linkages. Spring patterns showed that administrators acted as communication intermediaries for only 45 percent of the faculty, but by fall this assistance was provided to over 80 percent.

Collegial norms thus provide further evidence of principals' deliberate action to reduce uncertainty about teachers' success with students and to increase consensus about the importance and capability of being successful. Through norms of collegiality, principals wield the power of peers' collective perception.

Teacher Evaluation

The psychic rewards of teaching depend considerably on demonstrable proof that students have learned. Yet many teachers indicate difficulty in knowing precisely how well they are doing (Ashton, Webb, and Doda 1983; Glidewell et al. 1983; Lortie 1975). Ambiguity in role performance in ineffective schools springs from at least two sources: the absence of clear guidelines about what teachers are to emphasize and the absence of clear criteria by which teachers are to be monitored and evaluated.

Ineffective inner-city principals, uncertain that their actions will produce any desirable effect, appear to muster little effort to resolve this ambiguity for teachers (see, for example, CSDE 1980; Levy 1970; Morris et al. 1981; Natriello 1984). Affirming this point is an NEA survey in which fewer than 50 percent of the randomly sampled principals reported having sufficient time to assess teachers accurately (Dreeben 1970). In fact, 33 percent of the tenured teachers and 19 percent of the probationary teachers reported no classroom observation at all (Dreeben 1970; see also Dornbusch and Scott 1975; Natriello 1984). An even gloomier picture of teacher evaluation is painted by Natriello and Dornbusch (1980–81). In their sample, teachers reported receiving formal evaluations from their supervisors only once every three years. Commented one teacher, "If I were to drop dead, the only way they could find out would be the smell after a few days" (Natriello and Dornbusch 1980–81).

Of equal concern to teachers in the management of uncertainty are the criteria used for evaluation. Other NEA surveys (Weisenstein 1976) reveal that in evaluating teachers, principals periodically (although seldom regularly) use checklists to record their impressions of a teacher's mastery of certain characteristics or skills (such as personal appearance, lesson planning, speaking voice, classroom control). Such evaluations may include subjective rating systems and criteria with no known empirical connection to student achievement. Raters with differing perspectives may record quite different responses, and observations of varying frequency and length are likely to produce quite different perceptions. Where one principal sees tedious repetition, another may see proper overlearning and pacing.

Teachers who report being unaware of the criteria used to evaluate them are strongly dissatisfied—a condition that characterized about half the teachers in Natriello and Dornbusch's study. In discussing their findings, Natriello and Dornbusch note that teachers who are unaware of the standards used to evaluate them are in no position to redirect their energies toward improvement. Another significant result is their striking finding that receipt of negative evaluation is unrelated to teacher satisfaction. Clearly, then, teachers who believe that their principals see them regularly and base evaluations on understood criteria find inspiration for improvement regardless of the sentiment expressed in the evaluation.

In stark contrast to schools where teacher uncertainty arises from infrequent, unclear supervision (if, indeed, any supervision at all), principals or their administrative assistants in effective schools are ubiquitous in their efforts to monitor classroom affairs (Armor et al. 1976; Brookover et al. 1979; CSDE 1980; Coulson 1977; Phi Delta Kappa 1980; Rutter et al. 1979; Sizemore, Brossard, and Harrigan 1983; Wellisch et al. 1978) and student achievement within them (CSDE 1980; Glenn and McLean 1981; Phi Delta Kappa 1980; Sizemore, Brossard, and Harrigan 1983; Spartz et al. 1977; Venezky and Winfield 1979; Weber 1971; Wynne 1980). In response to limited progress, additional assistance (that is, support help) is often dispatched to needy classrooms (Armor et al. 1976; CSDE 1980; Phi Delta Kappa 1980; Rutter et al. 1979; Sizemore, Brossard, and Harrigan 1983; Venezky and Winfield 1979; Weber 1971).

When teachers are regularly observed, they develop new skills. In a longitudinal study of beginning elementary teachers, Turner (1965) found that greater skill acquisition by teachers in both reading and arithmetic instruction was primarily a function of the amount of supervision they received. Teachers who report frequent evaluations by their principals believe them better able to judge the quality of their work (Natriello and Dornbusch 1980–81) and to help them acquire new skills (Natriello 1984). The result of teachers' skill acquisition, of course, is greater effectiveness in the classroom and so larger psychic dividends. Not surprisingly, then, frequency of evaluation is correlated quite strongly with teachers' commitment to the school (Azumi and Madhere 1983; Chapman and Lowther 1982; Dornbusch and Scott 1975; Natriello and Dornbusch 1980–81).

In addition to teachers' professional development, active monitoring in the effective school serves several vital functions. First, it serves as a continual academic signal to staff about the priorities of the school and the importance of their individual contributions in achieving them. Second, it provides a clear basis for decision making within the school. Third, it establishes standards for knowing when goals have been attained. Fourth, it informs all who work within the school precisely what constitutes acceptable performance.

The interactions within one effective school described in the Phi Delta Kappa study (1980, chap. 2) are illustrative. The principal called initial meetings with small groups of teachers at each grade level to discuss and formulate specific instructional objectives and to determine how to meet them. As a result, 85 percent of the faculty reported knowing exactly what was expected of them, and 100 percent felt that additional help was available if needed. In subsequent meetings held with the entire faculty, achievement-test scores were analyzed in an effort to diagnose reasons for any lack of academic progress.

Azumi and Madhere's (1983) study of fifty-two urban elementary schools provides additional insight into the interrelationships of teacher evaluation, certainty about professional practice, and student achievement. Path analysis revealed that frequency of observational feedback from administrators or colleagues combined with teacher certainty accounts for 30 percent of the variation in student achievement between schools, if school SES and teacher experience are held constant. In turn, feedback accounted for 27 percent of the variance in teachers' certainty that they could bring about improved student achievement.

Clearly, the feedback mechanism of the effective school keeps staff from suffering uncertainty. Obtaining information on the outputs of teaching, comparing these outputs against the standards prescribed by goals, detecting significant departures from the standards, and issuing technical assistance and directives back to the staff to improve on the quality of outputs suggest a taut system wherein teacher uncertainty is minimized.

Buffering the Technical Core

In their efforts to accrue psychic rewards, teachers often indict classroom or school managerial tasks as an almost overwhelming handicap (Bredeson, Fruth, and Kasten 1983). Lortie (1975), for instance, found that the most frequently cited irritants to teachers in their push for greater productivity involved "down time," when teachers were pulled off task to attend to some relatively trivial administrative matter.

Not surprisingly, interruptions to the flow of teaching occur more frequently in some schools than in others. In the unsuccessful urban school studied by Levy, for example, teachers were barraged with so much paperwork that it appeared that collecting data was "the school's only task and the teacher's only duty" (Levy 1970, p. 112). When asked, teachers invariably voice the opinion that the primary function of nonteaching school personnel should be to remove obstacles that stand in the way of their teaching (Leacock 1969; Lortie 1975).

Studies linking engaged time to student learning (for example, Stallings 1980) bear out the importance of this intuitively reasonable proposition. Organizational theorists also confirm its wisdom. Managers, who have the greatest stake in the survival of an organization, attempt to "buffer" the technical core to reduce external uncertainty and hence augment the possibilities for rational action (Thompson 1967). That is, organizational buffering occurs in an effort to reduce to a minimum the extraneous forces that may upset the pursuit of operational goals. It is important to note, however, that buffering occurs most frequently and with the greatest success where there is clear understanding of the cause-effect relationship between goals and means to reach them (Thompson 1967). In other words, protecting the technical core of an organization makes sense only where there is certainty that particular actions (that is, teaching) produce the desired outcome (that is, learning).

If the presence of buffering strategies depends in large measure on the absence of uncertainty, it comes as no surprise to learn that teachers in effective schools are buffered by administrators to a far greater extent than teachers in ineffective schools. In effective schools, for example, principals attend to the material requirements and organization of instructional programs (Armor et al. 1976; Hunter 1979; Phi Delta Kappa 1980; Sizemore, Brossard, and Harrigan 1983; Spartz et al. 1977; Venezky and Winfield 1979; Wellisch et al. 1978), provide clerical assistance for routine paperwork (Rutter et al. 1979), and mobilize outside resources to assist teachers with nonteaching tasks (Hunter 1979; Phi Delta Kappa 1980; Venezky and Winfield 1979).

Effective principals also buffer teachers' time. Classroom time is protected from frequent interruptions such as loudspeaker announcements (Stallings 1980; Fisher et al. 1980), school assemblies (Rutter et al. 1979), and other low-priority, intrusive events (Armor et al. 1976; Glenn and McLean 1981; Sizemore, Brossard, and Harrigan 1983). Given the positive relationship between engaged time and learning, there is clear logic behind this buffering strategy; committing a larger portion of the school day to uninterrupted teaching increases the certainty of higher student achievement (Coleman et al. 1982; Rutter et al. 1979). Although it seems obvious that teachers burdened by insufficient resources cannot function effectively, the apparent lack of attention to these administrative details by ineffective principals (Armor et al. 1976; Rutter et al. 1979; Venezky and Winfield 1979) again denotes their absence of certainty about teachers' capacity to help students learn.

Still another buffering strategy employed by effective principals provides order through formalization. Formalization is said to exist where rules and procedures are specified to handle most behavioral contingencies. Teachers act in certain ways because there is clear delineation of tasks among staff members (Armor et al. 1976; Sizemore, Brossard, and Harrigan 1983; Wellisch et al. 1978). Formalization, then, predates any technical activity in order of priority and ensures (to the extent that rules are enforced consistently) the orderly behavior of school staff.

With respect to policies and practices regarding student discipline, effective urban principals set clear expectations in the form of rules, directives, and specification of penalties (Brookover et al. 1979; Rutter et al. 1979; Sizemore, Brossard, and Harrigan 1983; Weber 1971; Wynne 1980). These policies are enforced consistently throughout the school by both administrators and teachers (Morris 1982; Rutter et al. 1979; Wynne 1980). Thus, formalization provides a context in which all actors in the school know precisely how they are expected to behave. Greater formalization results, among other things, in teachers' experiencing less role strain (that is, strain felt from having to fulfill incompatible role obligations, such as teaching versus disciplining) and also greater satisfaction in teaching, since, as many researchers have noted, orderly students learn more than those who are not (Fisher et al. 1980; Good and Grouws 1977; Stallings 1980). Formalization as a buffering strategy, therefore, shows clear logic.

A word of caution, however. It is clear from the body of findings on formalization that the uncertainty of organizational participants sometimes produces overconformity and rigidity (Scott 1981). In other words, with too little certainty, organizations can seek to buffer their technical core through both excessive pressures for conformity and excessive specification of rules and regulations. The costs of organizational rigidity, however, are high. Insistence on ritualistic adherence to school rules may lead to teachers feeling strongly dissatisfied with their work (Hoy, Tarter, and Forsyth 1978; Morris 1982), to higher anxiety and tension (Miskel, Fevurly, and Stewart 1979), to goal displacement (Willower and Jones 1963), and to greater feelings of powerlessness (Cox and Wood 1980). Particularly when increased formalization threatens technical autonomy, reductions in teacher effectiveness may result (CSDE 1980; Coates and Thoresen 1978).

It is precisely at this point that schools face a critical dilemma (Scott 1981). If they allow too much freedom for their faculty members, they are apt to confront erratic and sometimes organizationally irrelevant behavior. If they allow too little freedom for their faculty members, they are likely to produce oppressed, alienated, or bureaucratic teachers who are unproductive, also. Effective schools, as shall be seen next, solve the predicament by coupling high formalization at the managerial level with low formalization at the technical level.

Participation in Decision Making

Frequently found in effective schools, and another way in which goal consensus is achieved, is the joint participation of administration and staff in technical decision making, that is, selecting instructional materials, determining appropriate instructional methods and techniques, establishing general instructional policies, and so forth (Armor et al. 1976; CSDE 1980; Glenn and McLean 1981; Rutter et al. 1979; Wynne 1980; Wellisch et al. 1978; Phi Delta Kappa 1980). Teachers' willingness to participate in technical decision making, it should be recognized, denotes adoption of school goals. Of equal importance, colleagues in effective schools interact in making technical decisions.

Decision Making and Teacher Performance

For competent teachers, in work tied directly to students, greater expenditures of effort always leads to greater psychic rewards (Lortie 1975; Stark et al. 1980). Teachers contribute willingly if they are certain their efforts will result in demonstrable classroom benefits. Not surprisingly, several studies identified effective schools (Armor et al. 1976; CSDE 1980; Glenn and McLean 1981; Hunter 1979; Phi Delta Kappa 1980; Weber 1971) as those that encouraged teachers to adapt or modify schoolwide instructional programs to the individual classroom. Indeed, in the most effective school studied by Sizemore, Brossard, and Harrigan (1983), the principal bucked district-office policy so that teachers could use materials they found most effective. Not unexpectedly, in all of these studies the increased pertinence of instructional programs to students' particular needs resulted in greater skill acquisition overall.

The performance benefits of collective decision making may result from the deliberate evaluation, suggestions, discussion, and modifications that are necessary to improve the quality of academic programs. These in turn lead to teachers' increased clarity about instructional purpose and method and, in the end, to increased instructional effectiveness. Decisions become conscious, well-reasoned choices rather than arbitrary or automatic reactions. Studies of teachers' role ambiguity support this notion. Mohrman, Cooke, and Mohrman (1979), in a study of 460 midwestern elementary and high school teachers, found that those who participated in technical decision making also experienced less role ambiguity. This in turn reduced teachers' uncertainty and increased their satisfaction in relations with their superiors (see also Keith 1979; Schwab and Iwanicki 1982). Azumi and Madhere's (1983) data also show that teachers who have less input in the setting of instructional policy have greater uncertainty about their capacity to bring about improvements in student performance. The products of uncertainty, of course, weigh heavily on the acquisition of teaching rewards.

Decision Making and Ownership

At the symbolic level, participation in technical decision making increases teachers' sense of ownership of school instructional goals and buys them a stake in the future of a collective enterprise. Ownership of school programs, therefore, seems critical for two reasons. First, student achievement suffers at the hands of teachers who are not committed to the program they teach (CSDE 1980; McLaughlin and Marsh 1978). Second, collective ownership permits administrative coordination of schoolwide instructional programs, a characteristic frequently cited in the distinction between effective and ineffective schools (CSDE 1980; Glenn and McLean 1981; Hunter 1979; Sizemore, Brossard, and Harrigan 1983; Venezky and Winfield 1979; Weber 1971).

On the latter point, continual student progress is less assured in the absence of a well-articulated program. In poorly coordinated programs, teachers may be reluctant to pace students by their rate of skill acquisition if the new material to be learned infringes on the domain of succeeding grade levels. Moreover, student learning tends to be fragmented from one grade level to the next if curricular materials do not build serially in an ever-widening understanding of important skills and concepts.

It is important to note that the articulation of classrooms into coherent, schoolwide programs implies a process of continual development resulting from, and enabled by, the commitment of a stable staff of administrators and teachers. The most effective inner-city schools studied by Venezky and Winfield (1979) and by Weber (1971) had developed their reading programs over a three- to nine-year period. Further, although several years are required to effectively "debug" a curriculum, most schools change basic instructional packages at least once every four years or have several different programs operating simultaneously (Venezky and Winfield 1979). Teachers may be reluctant to contribute personal resources if a program is replaced frequently, or if their own continued commitment to the school is in question.

In review, teacher participation in technical decision making is the stuff of collegial interaction. Participation implies a commitment to school-based instructional programs, better curriculum development through the adaptation of curricular material to specific classroom needs, and increased student learning resulting from greater teacher effectiveness. The end result for teachers may be additional psychic benefits.

LEARNING TO TEACH (AND TO TEACH BETTER)

Thus far I have described how the effective principal acts to reduce the degree of uncertainty confronting teachers, thereby enhancing their capacity for rational planning and action. However, as harmful as uncertainty is to rational action, there is an equal danger in too much certainty. When organizational participants program themselves out of challenging and new situations, they tend to become bored and lose interest. Thus, a central challenge confronting all effective schools is to find levels that are just right in their balance between security and stimulation (Scott 1981).

Effective schools meet this challenge through a combination of formal and informal mechanisms that define "good teaching," accentuate the importance of ongoing skill acquisition, define the standards by which teachers measure their success in teaching, signal the need to develop new teaching skills, and provide ways to learn and improve. However, clearer meaning can be given to norms that stress continual improvement by returning to the earlier distinction between isolated and collegial settings, for nowhere is the contrast between ineffective and effective schools more profound than in the process of learning to teach.

Although teachers vary in academic and experiential preparation prior to service, neophytes in any type of school usually feel wholly unprepared for the realities they encounter with their first class of students (Coates and Thoreson 1978; Fuller 1969; Leacock 1969; McArthur 1978; Purcell and Seifert 1982). Indeed, when experienced teachers look back upon their formal preservice training, the majority of them remember their education course work as too theoretical and not sufficiently practical (Dreeben 1970; Lortie 1975).

"Reality shock" may describe the experiences of new entrants, as idealism and romanticism give way to understanding that before one can teach students anything, it is necessary for them to be attentive (McArthur 1978). Managing student behavior is the first important task of new teachers. Moreover, as noted earlier, control of student behavior is a central element in the social system of the school and, as such, is used as an early measure of the entrants' teaching potential by the principal, fellow faculty (Leacock 1969; Warren 1975; Willower and Jones 1963), and the beginning teachers themselves (Hoy 1969; Leacock 1969). Yet classroom discipline seems to depend heavily on the establishment of orderly conditions at the school level.

Thus, the acquisition of skills related to teaching, the type of skills that one acquires, and the extent of one's potential skill development all depend in large measure on the school's prevailing norms and patterns of interaction. Within isolated settings, strong norms of autonomy militate against requests for and offers of assistance among colleagues, in part because both are perceived as statements about relative status (Lortie 1975). In the study by Glidewell and colleagues (1983), for example, teachers' commitment to the norm of autonomy operated to (a) reduce their perceived need for advice and support and (b) mitigate against their requesting and offering advice, even in settings such as teacher centers that were established for precisely those purposes.

Trial-and-Error Learning

With norms of autonomy mediating against asking for help and with the possible risks of having their inadequacies exposed, the beginning teacher's skill acquisition in isolated settings is limited almost entirely to trial-and-error learning. Not unexpectedly, two-thirds of the teachers in Lortie's (1975) Five Towns sample reported that experience was their major means for learning to teach (see also Leacock 1969).

However, a number of problems arise for neophytes who rely almost exclusively on trial-and-error learning (Lortie 1975). First, they are limited in their possibilities for success by their own personal ability to discern problems, develop alternative solutions, choose among them, and assess outcomes. Second, in selecting standards of teaching excellence toward which to strive, neophytes typically fall back upon their recollections of former teachers from their own student days, rather than seek models of excellence among thier colleagues. Third, the absence of a consensually developed technology of teaching in the isolated setting limits the neophyte's likelihood of learning any preexisting body of practical knowledge. Without such knowledge, beginners are less able to perceive and interpret daily events and critical transactions, which might be easily understood if they had access to an already developed discourse. Each teacher, then, must construct anew for himself or herself a conception of professional excellence and a manner in which to attain it.

Without benefit of positive collegial exchange or administrative support and feedback and with strong external pressure from peers and the principal, who push custodial control of students, beginning teachers in isolated work settings either defect (Bredeson, Fruth, and Kasten 1983; Chapman and Hutcheson 1982; Dworkin 1980; Leacock 1969; Paschal and Treloar 1979; Willower and Jones 1963) or move toward adopting the school's subcultural values (Leacock 1969; Paschal and Treloar 1979; Willower and Jones 1963). More-liberal and permissive views, which stress the importance of each student's individuality and the development of a classroom climate geared to meeting a wide range of student needs, give way—usually within the first year—to a custodial view, wherein the maintenance of order is stressed, students are distrusted, and a punitive, moralistic orientation toward control predominates (Ashton, Webb, and Doda 1983; Day 1959; Hoy 1969; Leacock 1969; Levy 1970). It is the rare teacher who keeps faith in his or her ideals when those surrounding him or her advise otherwise.

Teachers' subsequent skill mastery in isolated settings appears equally constrained by norms of the scope and nature of collegial interaction. In the urban elementary school that Warren (1975) studied, for example, the reading specialist was instructed by the principal to wait for an invitation from teachers to demonstrate alternative methods of teaching reading. Although the waiting strategy conformed to prevailing school norms, it did not produce invitations (see also Armor et al. 1976; CSDE 1980). Thus, in isolated settings it is highly unlikely that teachers who need the most help receive it.

In further support of this point is evidence of a curvilinear relationship between teacher experience and student achievement, with effectiveness beginning to decline after five years (Katzman 1971; McLaughlin and Marsh 1978; Murnane 1975). In other words, restricted to trial-and-error learning, there may be a ceiling effect on the individual's capacity to grow in the absence of others' professional input. This limited opportunity for skill development in turn reduces teachers' chances to acquire intrinsic rewards and is therefore a good predictor of low commitment (Bredeson, Fruth, and Kasten 1983; Chapman and Lowther 1982; Litt and Turk 1983).

Norms of Continual Improvement

Effective schools, in contrast, promote norms of continual improvement. Here it is assumed that improvement of teaching is a collective rather than solo enterprise, and that analysis, evaluation, and experimentation in concert with one's colleagues set the conditions under which teachers become more effective (Little 1982). In these settings, inexperienced teachers have far less reason to cover up their mistakes from colleagues. In fact, inexperienced teachers have reason not to isolate their mistakes. For one thing, responsibilities to one's colleagues direct beginners to become as effective teachers as possible. Additionally, neophytes maximize their own rewards when they seek out the advice and assistance of others. If improvement in teaching results from collegial exchange, beginners stand to profit directly from the suggestions of others.

In testing whether the work setting determines the degree to which new teachers engage in task-related exchange, Bishop found that those from collegial settings engaged in substantially more work, as well as friendship, associations than did those from isolated settings (Bishop 1977). This greater interaction could be expected to produce greater classroom effectiveness.

Bishop found the setting also determined to some degree the work orientations of beginning teachers. While neophytes in isolated settings developed a custodial student-control ideology, new teachers in collegial settings maintained more humanistic work orientations, and gave importance to tending to the individual needs of students (see also Ashton, Webb, and Doda 1983). The emphasis in collegial settings on teachers' skill development and on school-enforced standards for student behavior may provide beginners with sufficient support to avoid becoming custodians. Thus, the organizational context of work appears to be a good predictor of the degree of "reality shock" and role conflict that beginners first suffer. These in turn affect their acquisition of psychic rewards.

A third noteworthy finding of Bishop's study deals with the role of teacher experience. While the amount of task-related discussion increased with teachers' experience in collegial settings, in isolated settings there was a substantial decline in collegial exchange with experience. This curious finding (although escaping the attention of Bishop) may perhaps be explained by differences in the product of collegial exchange in different work contexts. The reader will recall the tendency of teachers in isolated settings to engage in experience swapping as a means of gaining support, whereas in collegial settings teachers more readily requested and gave advice and assistance. Thus, while the product of exchange in isolated settings is often sympathy, the product of exchange in collegial settings is often ideas. Ideas in turn give rise to greater experimentation in collegial settings (Bishop 1977; Cohen 1981; Little 1982). Further, if experimentation in collegial settings leads to increased effectiveness, the resulting rewards of teaching will reinforce and increase task-related collegial interaction.

The importance of normative climate to teachers' ongoing professional development is also poignantly illustrated in the study by Glidewell and colleagues (1983). For more-experienced teachers, repeated task-related interaction with colleagues increased their beliefs about the availability of professional knowledge and their certainty about the technology of teaching.

Equally significant, norms of collegiality and certainty about the technology of teaching increased teachers' need for support and requests for and offers of assistance, while norms of autonomy and uncertainty about the technology of teaching greatly reduced teachers' need for support and offers and requests. In essence, teachers continue to ask for assistance from and offer assistance to colleagues when they believe it will help them improve.

Two additional studies permit a more detailed examination of the relationship between task-related collegial exchange and teachers' skill acquisition and development. Ashton, Webb, and Doda (1983) compared an isolated with a collaborative urban school by both surveying and observing teachers on the effective teaching behaviors identified by Good and Grouws (1977). Compared to their counterparts in the isolated setting, teachers in the collegial setting were less custodial in their treatment of lower achievers, more certain about their capacity to affect student learning, and consequently more likely to display effective teaching behaviors. Further, Griffin and colleagues (1983), in their longitudinal study of teacher training, found that the degree of collaborative relations between cooperating and student teachers predicted increases in the effective teaching behaviors of both groups.

Implied in the operation of collegial norms is a marked increase in informal evaluations by one's peers. Although in isolated settings the evaluations by staff external to the classroom (that is, principal and colleagues) are almost never used by teachers as indicators of their effectiveness (Lortie 1975), the situation is altogether different in collaborative settings. Here, teachers feel strongly that colleagues have a right to evaluate fellow teachers and that collegial feedback is generally sound (Cohen 1981). Indeed, experimental studies show that teachers can, with a modicum of feedback, learn effective teaching strategies with subsequent payoffs of increased student achievement (Anderson, Evertson, and Brophy 1979; Good and Grouws 1977; Stallings 1980). Thus, if collegial evaluation and feedback result in teachers' improved performance, intrinsic rewards accrue to both teacher-learner and teacher-instructor.

Fruitful collegial exchange, then, recycles synergistically. Here it is seen most clearly that some organizational climates foster teachers' skill acquisition and development more than others. Collegial norms represent a form of group problem solving, social support, and ongoing professional development. As new ideas are infused into the network, alternative and better solutions to classroom problems are found. In essence, good teachers working with other good teachers get even better.

It is therefore my sense that effective teachers are "made" rather than "born"; that they develop, perfect, and add to their fund of teaching skills throughout their professional careers; and that their continual skill acquisition and development is a necessary precondition to survival in the profession without frustration and dissatisfaction.

A CAUTION ABOUT, AND SUMMARY OF, THE ANALYSIS

Before reviewing the school-level processes that govern and shape teacher behavior, an important caution seems warranted. The characteristics of effective elementary schools serving poor minority students may not generalize to other school populations or even to higher grade levels. The phenomenon of tight coupling may, in fact, be a direct function of the specific population and grade levels served (see, for example, Firestone and Wilson 1984). For one thing, basic skill acquisition is the curricular province of the elementary school. Elementary teachers, unlike their secondary counterparts, are trained to accept this responsibility, and curricular materials have been designed with this function in mind. That the urban poor experience difficulty in basic skill acquisition at the elementary school level may underscore both the importance of this knowledge as a schoolwide goal and the appropriate pride in reaching it (see Lortie 1975; Plihal 1982). In contrast, middle-class elementary schools, with the problems and goals of positive desegregated elementary schools, have more-diversified objectives than schools serving primarily low-income black youngsters. Goals of competing importance decrease the likelihood that consensus about their priority will develop. Similarly, the emphasis placed on disciplinary standards in the effective urban school may be seen as a rational response to a problem perhaps not experienced to the same extent by middle-class schools. Because faculty in middle-class schools may not be mobilized in a common purpose, then, there may be less internal connectedness. Mindful that findings on effective schools may be conditioned by characteristics of the clientele served, a schematic representation of critical school processes is offered in Figure 9–1.

Principal   Goals   Principal action: Group cohesiveness
certainty→ achievement → teacher recruitment, → teachers' collaborative →
                               buffering the   decision making, problem
                               technical core,   solving, and
                               performance   experimentation
                               monitoring and
                               assistance

               Teacher → Success → Teacher
               certainty   and rewards   commitment

Figure 9–1
Explaining School Success

In explaining school success, I place heavy emphasis on the ideas of certainty and organizational goals. School excellence results from rational planning and action with which principals, because of their certainty that excellence can be achieved, mobilize teachers against a single common enemy: low student achievement. To bring about basic-skills acquisition, effective principals develop common objectives for their schools, which staff will collectively accomplish with a full command of teaching strategies developed through collaborative efforts; with maximum time, materials, and technical assistance to implement them; and with professional confidence that school failure can and should be abolished. With common objectives come clear directions toward which teachers point their energies for improvement, shared reason for professional dialogue among teachers, a basis for knowing when their efforts have succeeded, and collectively issued recognition for progress made.

What sets the effective inner-city school apart from others is, first, that staff members' personal motives are congruent with the goals of the organization. Induction into teaching in the effective school sets the conditions under which goal consensus is achieved and decides the means to reach them. Second, common beliefs or values carry the weight of organizational authority and control. Since values represent group consensus as well as personal commitment, there is a binding—if not moral—aspect to them that forms the basis of social control and reduces the possibility of opportunistic behavior (Scott 1981). That is, actions that contribute to the attainment of goals are the essential things of value, and, as such, form the basis for solidarity and legitimacy within the school community. Finally, as a product of actions to attain goals such as performance auditing and problem solving, efficacious technologies develop. The technology of teaching that is passed along to new recruits then circles back to provide organizational participants with inducements that encourage them to make contributions.

REFERENCES

Anderson, Linda; Evertson, Carolyn; and Brophy, Jere. "An Experimental Study of Effective Teaching in First-Grade Reading Groups." *Elementary School Journal* 79 (March 1979): 193–223.

Armor, David J.; Conry-Oseguera, Patricia; Cox, Millicent; King, Nicelma; McDonnell, Lorraine; Pascal, Anthony; Pauly, Edward; and Zellman, Gail. *Analysis of the School Preferred Reading Program in Selected Los Angeles Minority Schools.* Santa Monica, Calif.: Rand Corp., 1976.

Ashton, Patricia T.; Webb, Rodman B.; and Doda, Nancy. *A Study of Teachers' Sense of Efficacy: Final Report.* Gainesville: University of Florida, Foundations of Education, 1983.

Azumi, Jann E., and Madhere, Serge. "Professionalism, Power and Performance: The Relationships between Administrative Control, Teacher Conformity, and Student Achievement." Paper presented at the Annual Meeting of the American Educational Research Association, Montreal, April 1983.

Bishop, James M. "Organizational Influences on the Work Orientations of Elementary Teachers." *Sociology of Work and Occupation* 4, no. 2 (1977): 171–208.

Bredeson, Paul V.; Fruth, Marvin J.; and Kasten, Kathrine L. "Organizational Incentives and Secondary School Teaching." *Journal of Research and Development in Education* 16, no. 4 (1983): 52–56.

Bridges, Edwin M., and Hallinan, Maureen T. "Subunit Size, Work System Interdependence, and Employee Absenteeism." *Educational Administration Quarterly* 14, no. 2 (1978): 24–42.

Brookover, Wilbur; Beady, Charles; Flood, Patricia; Schweitzer, John; and Wisenbaker, Joe. *School Social Systems and Student Achievement: Schools Can Make a Difference.* New York: Praeger, 1979.

California State Department of Education (CSDE). *Report on the Special Studies of Selected ECE Schools with Increasing and Decreasing Reading Scores.* Sacramento, Calif.: Office of Program Evaluation and Research, 1980.

Chapman, David W., and Hutcheson, Sigrid M. "Attrition from Teaching Careers: A Discriminant Analysis." *American Educational Research Journal* 19 (1982): 93–106.

Chapman, David W., and Lowther, Malcolm A. "Teachers' Satisfaction with Teaching." *Journal of Educational Research* 75, no. 4 (1982): 240–47.

Charters, W. W., Jr. "Stability and Change in the Communication Structure of School Faculties." *Educational Administration Quarterly* 5, no. 3 (1969): 15–38.

Coates, Thomas J., and Thoresen, Carl E. "Teacher Anxiety: A Review with Recommendations." *Review of Educational Research* 46 (Spring 1978): 159–84.

Cohen, Elizabeth G. "Sociology Looks at Team Teaching." *Research in Sociology of Education and Socialization* 2 (1981): 163–93.

Coleman, James S.; Hoffer, Thomas; and Kilgore, Sally. *Public and Private Schools* (draft). Chicago: National Opinion Research Center, University of Chicago, 1982.

Coulson, John E. *Overview of the National Evaluation of the Emergency School Aid Act.* Santa Monica, Calif.: System Development Corp., 1977.

Cox, Harold, and Wood, James R. "Organizational Structure and Professional Alienation: The Case of Public School Teachers." *Peabody Journal of Education* 58, no. 1 (1980): 1–6.

Day, Harry P. "Attitude Changes of Beginning Teachers after Initial Teaching Experience." *Journal of Teacher Education* 10 (September 1959): 326–28.

Dornbusch, Sanford M., and Scott, W. Richard. *Evaluation and the Exercise of Authority.* San Francisco, Calif.: Jossey-Bass, 1975.

Dreeben, Robert. *The Nature of Teaching.* Glenview, Ill.: Scott, Foresman and Co., 1970.

Dworkin, Anthony G. "The Changing Demography of Public School Teachers: Some Implications for Faculty Turnover in Urban Areas." *Sociology of Education* 53 (April 1980): 65–73.

Firestone, William A., and Wilson, Bruce L. *Using Bureaucratic and Cultural Linkages to Improve Instruction: The High School Principal's Contribution.* Eugene: University of Oregon, Center for Educational Policy and Management, 1984.

Fisher, Charles W.; Berliner, David C.; Filby, Nikola; Marliave, Richard; Cahan, Leonard S.; and Dishaw, Marilyn. "Teaching Behaviors, Academic Learning Time, and Student Achievement: An Overview." In *Time to Learn*, edited by Carolyn Denham and Ann Lieberman. Washington, D.C.: Department of Education, 1980.

Fuller, Frances F. "Concerns of Teachers: A Developmental Conceptualization." *American Educational Research Journal* 6 (March 1969): 207–226.

Glenn, Beverly C., and McLean, Taylor. *What Works? An Examination of Effective Schools for Poor Black Children.* Cambridge, Mass.: Harvard University, Center for Law and Education, 1981.

Glidewell, John C.; Tucker, S.; Todt, M.; and Cox, S. "Professional Support Systems: The Teaching Profession." In *Applied Research in Help-seeking and Reactions to Aid*, edited by A. Madler, J. D. Fisher, and B. M. DePaulo. New York: Academic Press, 1983.

Good, Thomas L., and Grouws, Douglas. "Teaching Effects: A Process-Product Study in Fourth-grade Mathematics Classrooms." *Journal of Teacher Education* 28 (May/June 1977): 49–54.

Griffin, Gary A.; Barnes, Susan J.; Hughes, Robert, Jr.; O'Neal, Sharon; Defino, Maria E.; Edwards, Sara A.; and Hukill, Hobart. *Clinical Preservice Teacher Education: Final Report.* Austin: University of Texas Press, 1983.

Hoy, Wayne K. "Pupil Control Ideology and Organizational Socialization: A Further Examination of the Influence of Experience on the Beginning Teacher." *School Review* 77 (September/December 1969): 257–265.

Hoy, Wayne K.; Tarter, C. J.; and Forsyth, Patrick. "Administrative Behavior and Subordinate Loyalty: An Empirical Assessment." *Journal of Educational Administration* 16, no. 1 (1978): 29–38.

Hunter, M. G. *Final Report of the Michigan Cost-Effectiveness Study*. East Lansing: Michigan Department of Education, 1979.

Katzman, Michael T. *The Political Economy of Urban Schools*. Cambridge, Mass.: Harvard University Press, 1971.

Keith, Pat M. "Correlates of Role Strain in the Classroom." *Urban Education* 14, no. 1 (1979): 19–30.

Leacock, Eleanor. *Teaching and Learning in City Schools*. New York: Basic Books, 1969.

Levy, Gerald E. *Ghetto School: Class Warfare in an Elementary School*. Indianapolis: Western Publishing Co., 1970.

Litt, Mark D., and Turk, Dennis C. "Stress, Dissatisfaction, and Intention to Leave Teaching in Experienced Public High School Teachers." Paper presented at the Annual Meeting of the American Educational Research Association, Montreal, April 1983.

Little, Judith W. "Norms of Collegiality and Experimentation: Workplace Conditions of School Success." *American Educational Research Journal* 19, no. 3 (1982): 325–40.

Lortie, Dan C. "Observations on Teaching as Work." In *Second Handbook of Research on Teaching*, edited by R. M. Travers. Chicago: Rand McNally and Co., 1973.

Lortie, Dan C. *Schoolteacher: A Sociological Study*. Chicago: University of Chicago Press, 1975.

March, James G., and Simon, Herbert A. *Organizations*. New York: John Wiley and Sons, 1958.

McArthur, John T. "What Does Teaching Do to Teachers?" *Educational Administration Quarterly* 14, no. 3 (1978): 89–103.

McLaughlin, Milbrey W., and Marsh, David D. "Staff Development and School Change." *Teachers College Record* 80, no. 1 (1978): 69–94.

Miskel, Cecil G., Fevurly, Robert; and Stewart, John. "Organizational Structures and Processes, Perceived School Effectiveness, Loyalty, and Job Satisfaction." *Educational Administration Quarterly* 15, no. 3 (1979): 97–118.

Mohrman, Allan M.; Cooke, Robert A.; and Mohrman, Susan A. "Participation in Decision Making: A Multidimensional Perspective." *Educational Administration Quarterly* 15, no. 3 (1979): 97–113.

Morris, Monica B. *The Public School as Workplace: The Principal as a Key Element in Teacher Satisfaction. A Study of Schooling in the United States* (Technical Report Series, no. 32). Dayton, Ohio: Institute for Development of Educational Activities, 1982.

Morris, Van Cleve; Crowson, Robert L.; Hurwitz, Emanuel; and Porter-Gehrie, Cynthia. *The Urban Principal: Discretionary Decision-making in a Large Educational Organization*. Chicago: University of Illinois at Chicago, 1981.

Murnane, Richard J. *The Impact of School Resources on the Learning of Inner City Children.* Cambridge, Mass.: Ballinger Publishing Co., 1975.

Natriello, Gary. "Teachers' Perceptions of the Frequency of Evaluation and Assessments of Their Effort and Effectiveness." *American Educational Research Journal* 21, no. 3 (1984): 579–95.

Natriello, Gary, and Dornbusch, Sanford M. "Pitfalls in the Evaluation of Teachers by Principals." *Administrator's Notebook* 29, no. 6 (1980–81): 1–4.

Paschal, Billy J., and Treloar, James H. "A Longitudinal Study of Attitude Change in Prospective and Beginning Elementary School Teachers." *Teacher Educator* 15, no. 1 (1979): 2–9.

Phi Delta Kappa. *Why Do Some Urban Schools Succeed? The Phi Delta Kappa Study of Exceptional Urban Elementary Schools.* Bloomington, Ind.: Phi Delta Kappa, 1980.

Plihal, Jane. "Types of Intrinsic Rewards of Teaching and Their Relation to Teacher Characteristics and Variables in the Work Setting." Paper presented at the Annual Meeting of the American Educational Research Association, New York, 1982.

Purcell, Thomas D., and Seifert, Berniece B. "A Tri-State Survey of Student Teachers." *College Student Journal* 16 (Spring 1982): 27–29.

Rutter, Michael; Maughan, Barbara; Mortimore, Peter; and Ouston, Janet. *Fifteen Thousand Hours: Secondary Schools and Their Effect on Children.* Cambridge, Mass.: Harvard University Press, 1979.

Schwab, Richard L., and Iwanicki, Edward F. "Perceived Role Conflict, Role Ambiguity, and Teacher Burnout." *Educational Administration Quarterly* 19, no. 1 (1982): 60–74.

Scott, W. Richard. *Organizations: Rational, National, and Open Systems.* Englewood Cliffs, N. J.: Prentice-Hall, 1981.

Sizemore, Barbara; Brossard, Carlos A.; and Harrigan, Birney. *An Abashing Anomaly: The High Achieving Predominantly Black Elementary School* (final report). Pittsburgh: University of Pittsburgh, 1983.

Spartz, James L., et al. *Delaware Educational Accountability System Case Studies: Elementary School Grades 1–4.* Dover: Delaware Department of Public Instruction, 1977.

Spuck, Dennis W. "Reward Structures in the Public High School." *Educational Administration Quarterly* 10 (1974): 18–34.

Stallings, Jane. "Allocated Academic Learning Time Revisited, or Beyond Time on Task." *Educational Researcher* 9, no. 11 (1980): 11–16.

Stark, Joan S.; Austin, Anne E.; Lowther, Malcolm A.; Chapman, David W.; and Hutcheson, Sigrid M. *Teacher Certification Recipients at the University of Michigan, 1946 through 1976: A 1980 Follow-up Study.* Ann Arbor: University of Michigan, 1980. ED 209 209.

Thompson, James D. *Organizations in Action.* New York: McGraw-Hill Book Co., 1967.

Turner, Richard L. "Task Performance and Teaching Skill in the Intermediate Grades." *Journal of Teacher Education* 14 (September 1965): 299–307.

Tye, Kenneth A., and Tye, Barbara B. "Teacher Isolation and School Reform." *Phi Delta Kappan* 65 (January 1984): 319–322.

Venezky, Richard L., and Winfield, Linda F. *Schools That Succeed Beyond Expectations in Reading* (Studies on Education, Technical Report no. 1). Newark: University of Delaware, 1979.

Warren, Richard L. "Context and Isolation: The Teaching Experience in an Elementary School." *Human Organization* 34 (Summer 1975): 139–148.

Weber, George. *Inner-City Children Can Be Taught to Read: Four Successful Schools.* Washington, D.C.: Council for Basic Education, 1971.

Weisenstein, Greg R. "Teacher Evaluation: The Principal's Role." *OSSC Bulletin* 20 (1976): 3–23.

Wellisch, Jean B.; MacQueen, Anne H.; Carriere, Ronald A.; and Duck, Gary A. "School Management and Organization in Successful Schools." *Sociology of Education* 51 (July 1978): 211–226.

Willower, Donald J., and Jones, Ronald G. "When Pupil Control Becomes an Institutional Theme." *Phi Delta Kappan* 45 (November 1963): 107–109.

Wilson, Bruce L., and Corbett, H. Dickson. "Organization and Change: The Effects of School Linkages on the Quantity of Implementation." *Educational Administration Quarterly* 19, no. 4 (1983): 85–104.

Wynne, Edward A. *Looking at Schools: Good, Bad and Indifferent.* Lexington, Mass.: D.C. Heath & Co., 1980.